What people are sayi

"Judy Dragon and Terry Popp are d
understanding of multiplicity and th
pilation of personal stories, they have openeu up the world
giving the reader direct contact with the events that caused the fragmentation and the courage and dedication it took to dismantle the elaborate system. I have worked closely with them on a professional level and am inspired by their understanding and integrity."
 —*George J. Bilotta, Ph.D.* • *Executive Director of The Morris Center for*
Healing from Child Abuse, in San Francisco.

"Multiple Journeys to One brings us voices from far out on the spectrum of
abuse. The abuse, however, is not their entire story, for these are also testi-
monials to the courage, creativity, healing, strength and resiliency of the
human spirit. They are honest and compelling stories that underscore the
complex interplay of our bodies, psyches, and spirits. These are voices that
deserve to be heard. The stories offer rich and profound rewards to the reader."
 —*Paul Crissey* • *Board President of Survivorship, Past-President of the*
California Professional Society on the Abuse of Children, and former
Training Director of the California Consortium to Prevent Child Abuse.

"These firsthand accounts of horrific abuse demonstrate the flexibility of
the human mind when confronted with the will to live, its ability to shatter
in the process, and then recover back into wholeness. I recommend *Multiple
Journeys to One* to anyone interested in the mystery of human consciousness."
 —*Juliette Hanauer* • *Radio/TV talk show host. Documentary film maker.*

"Terry Popp and Judy Dragon have collected eight thoroughly engrossing
accounts of individuals struggling to overcome disastrous childhoods. The
stories and struggles are reminiscent of those I have heard in my office over
the past twenty-five years. One can only admire the courage and determination to get well that has been so aptly portrayed in this book."
 —*Dr. Robert S. Mayer* • *Nationally recognized authority on Multiple
Personality Disorder. Author of* Satan's Children: Case Studies in
Multiple Personality *and* Through Divided Minds.

"Terry Popp and Judy Dragon give us a direct experience of the world of
the multiple and of the long and often difficult journey towards integration
in this inspiring and life-affirming book. As therapists and teachers who
have spent many years working with subpersonalities, we feel that this work
is a real contribution both to the multiples and to the people who know them."
 —*Hal Stone, Ph.D.* and *Sidra Stone, Ph.D.* • *Co-creators of Voice Dialogue
and the Psychology of Selves. Authors of many books, including*
Embracing Our Selves: The Voice Dialogue Manual.

Multiple Journeys to One

Multiple Journeys to One

SPIRITUAL STORIES OF INTEGRATING FROM DISSOCIATIVE IDENTITY DISORDER

Foreword by Dr. Will Riggan

Edited by Judy Dragon & Terry Popp

Illustrations © _by_ Jonathan Rogers
Cover Design by Alexandra Hart
Cover Image by Paul Nicholson

Dancing Serpents Press

Published by:
DANCING SERPENTS PRESS
P. O. Box 8115, Santa Rosa, California 95407-1115
E-mail: danserpents@juno.com

Illustrations copyright © Jonathan Rogers

Library of Congress Catalog Card Number: 99-74441

This book is printed on acid-free paper
Printed by Patterson Printing, Benton Harbor, MI
Set in Berthold Baskerville typeface
Designed by Alexandra Hart,
Concepts Editorial & Design Services, Sebastopol, CA

ISBN 0-9672458-0-X
First Edition: July 1999

Theresa, with the clarity and groundedness of an ancient seer, viewed my experience as a cluster of stars whose coming together would form a super nova, whose light would become even stronger and brighter.
—Lindsey

Multiple Journeys to One
contains material some readers may find disturbing.
Please use discretion in reading this book.

Table of Contents

Foreword

G enerally the forums where Dissociative Identity Disorder (DID) is discussed, understood, and, in fact, defined, have been the exclusive domain of psychotherapists and psychiatrists. This situation is consistent with the implicit assumption that only the professional mental health community has the ability to evaluate and describe the etiology, the features, and the treatment modes of all mental/emotional disruptions. The claim to exclusivity is not helpful. I believe it to be of great importance to have those who know psychic distress from the inside weigh in with their insights in those same forums. The experiences of Vietnam veterans and of women in challenging and educating the therapeutic community about Posttraumatic Stress Disorder are cases in point. Thankfully, this has also been happening in the DID community.

In addition to gatherings and conferences organized and run by people recovering from the trauma which induced their DID, there is a small but growing library of their written work. *Multiple Journeys to One* makes a unique contribution to that library. It is the only book I know of written by survivors about one particular phenomenon in the healing process: integration. As a result, and not surprisingly, it also casts important new light on this aspect of healing DID.

Judy Dragon and Terry Popp set out to offer other survivors

some examples of the integration process, motivated in part by the absence from the literature of such help when they first went through that experience. By so doing, they and their contributors have done more. They have opened for reconsideration the meaning of integration and its timing as well. This has been accomplished without any attempt to present a cross-section of the DID population or to adhere to any other social science method. These were the stories they received in response to their call.

Integration is, as a rule, understood in the professional literature on DID to be a late step in the healing process, though not necessarily of the therapeutic process, and to mark the end of the fragmentation of the separate alters. However, what these authors have given us is a view of integration that is far more fluid and less certain in its import and meaning.

Clearly, all of the women in this volume are describing integrative experiences, the folding of alters into a larger consciousness. The fears and joys attending those experiences are quite vivid. It is also apparent from reading their stories that most do not exclude the possibility, or some even the likelihood, that there may be other alters, even other systems of alters, yet to be discovered. That does not diminish in any way the beauty and power of the integration they have already been through, and it frees us all, therapists, survivors, and family members alike, from the confines of believing that integration only happens once.

The editors have chosen, wisely I believe, to edit but not rewrite their contributors' chapters. What is lost in polish and writer's craft is offset by immediacy, personality, and, most dramatically, the common thread of strong spiritual connection. All took the great risk of exposing their hearts to create this book. All are to be commended for that, and all are to be congratulated on the results, especially Mss. Dragon and Popp.

—Will Riggan
December, 1998

Editors' Acknowledgments

I was at a 12-Step meeting in 1988, one I had rarely attended. Times were intense for me. I was experiencing an onslaught of new abuse memories. I was distancing from my husband of seventeen years. I was attempting to be present for my outer children and, at the same time, I worked at maintaining two careers. At the meeting, I spoke of feeling not in my body, of operating from my neck up, of hiding behind a facade that was crumbling. Looking around the room, I wondered if anyone could connect with my anguish and pain, and with the restructuring of the life I had once believed was real. There, on the other side of the room, nodding her head, was a vaguely familiar face—an attractive, alert, compassionate looking woman, maybe twenty years my senior. I knew I would talk to her after the meeting. She would understand.

Terry and I have been friends ever since. Back in 1988, we were starting to remember the involvement of our families in Satanic Ritual Abuse. We both felt isolated and traumatized. Within two months, we had formed a support group with four other women who had similar issues. We met twice a month for five years, crying, laughing, and holding each other. By sharing the feelings and memories of what had happened to us, we created a safe container to break the constraints of the cult programming. At the end of the five years, we felt the need to move out into the world in a different manner. The meetings were formally dissolved, though a few of us have remained in contact.

In the spring of 1995, Terry and I traveled to Sacramento to attend a survivors' meeting on Ritual Abuse and multiplicity. We had been out of touch for five or six months but, since the drive was long, had plenty of time to catch up. We discovered that in the intervening months both of us had integrated our many personalities. I had spoken to only one other integrated survivor. That conversation, several months earlier, after I integrated, led me to believe that my process was faulty, and that my feelings of shock, abandonment, and grief were off-base. I felt ashamed and alone. This person's integration had been a joyous event. Perhaps I had missed something. Perhaps I wasn't really integrated. My therapist recommended I be cautious whom I told about my vulnerable process. How comforting to find Terry, to know that someone I cared about and trusted had also gone through integration. In renewing our friendship, Terry and I continued our discussions about the commonalities and differences of our multiplicity and integration.

In the spring of 1996, one of my Inner Guides told me that I must write a book about my life. I had had similar messages in the past, but had ignored them. I wasn't a writer; I only wrote in my journal or produced small articles about abuse. However, I was definitely a networker and an organizer, having two years earlier created and produced a two-day healing symposium for our community. With these skills clearly accessible, I asked Terry to write a book with me about what abuse survivors experience in the process of integrating their multiple personalities. In the meantime, we presented our integration processes for local conferences on abuse and for groups of therapists. We felt a strong urge to let other survivors know that they need not feel alone while experiencing different levels of integration. We wanted to provide them with a sense of the reality of what was happening to them.

In finding the people who were willing to reveal, through the written word, their courageous journeys, this labor of love and healing was finally completed.

I thank my dear friend, Terry, for her gentle patience and scholarly expertise in teaching me to edit, and in supporting my growing abilities to write.

To my children: "When you are joyous, look deep into your heart, and you shall find it is only that which has given you sorrow that is giving you joy." —*Kahlil Gibran*

To my friends, therapists, and healers: Your loving belief in my truths and strangely attuned synchronicities has been the golden railings of light that supported my journey across the dark, mystical bridges. I keep crossing them.

To the writers: Your truths and courage set us all free to continue to be who we are at any given moment.

I would like to acknowledge the permission given to Terry and me by Shakti Gawain to quote from her book *Path of Transformation.*

With much gratitude, I also thank my persistent Inner Guiding Voices and the Creator who "loved" me into birthing this book.

—Judy Dragon
October 15, 1998

Working with Judy for the past two years to put together this book of remarkable stories from valiant, daring women has been exhilarating, frustrating, and, ultimately, immensely rewarding. I discovered more about the human spirit and the ingenuity of the creative mind from these women, and from Judy, than I gleaned from the dozens of books I had read on the subjects of multiplicity and childhood abuse.

I learned, again and again, that I have no control over anyone's life but my own—and that is frequently open to debate. My desire to adhere to a certain time line did not guarantee that others would have the same priority. My desire to present a book about multiples neatly integrated and fused, did not take into account the reality of the writers' worlds. Life is not neat and linear.

Most importantly, I learned that nothing in this world is static. I had heard over and over that "life is a process." It is, indeed. What I took for granted two years ago, I now know bears no relationship to the spiral-like continuity of a person's development. And hooray for that.

I thank my friends who put up with my retreats into isolation as I read through the manuscripts, fussing over each word and line. I feel truly blessed with their charity about my almost obsessive dedication to writing—my own, as well as that of others.

I thank my therapists: Maia for helping me to understand that the sacred has the capacity to carry within it the profane; Bill, who restored my faith in myself and my ability to heal.

I thank Judy for her quick and absorbent mind, and for being a true and compassionate friend. Without her inspiration, tenacity, and assistance, this book would never have been started, much less finished.

I thank our amazing writers for their patience, willingness, and generosity.

—Terry Popp
October 15, 1998

Introduction

Imagine awakening one morning to find thirty strangers in a house you assumed was yours alone. Imagine, further, that these strangers appear and disappear with alarming irregularity, stealing your valuables and taking with them time, memories, and feelings. Then imagine that they begin to inform you of events and experiences that cause your whole body to recoil. Are you having hallucinations? Going crazy? Having an emotional breakdown? Or are you becoming acquainted with the fact that you have DID, Dissociative Identity Disorder?

Dissociation is not an illness or disorder in itself; instead, it can be a child's reaction to a situation that threatens both the child's life and sanity. It is a coping mechanism that the person frequently must untangle later, if s/he is to live a full, fruitful life.

There are varying degrees of dissociation. A simplified way of understanding this complex phenomenon is to picture an arc. On the lower left hand side is the common dissociation and forgetfulness: everyone forgets, and then later remembers, things and events. The farther we go to the right of the continuum, however, the more the person is apt to dissociate at times of trauma and distress; parts split off creating fragments, or, sometimes, alter personalities.

[An alter is] an entity with a firm, persistent, and well-founded sense of self and a characteristic and consistent pattern of behavior and feelings in response to given stimuli. It must have a range of functions, a range of emotional responses, and a significant life history (of its own existence). (Kluft, 1984, p. 23, quoted in Putnam, *Diagnosis and Treatment of Multiple Personality Disorder*, 1989, p. 103)

Alter systems vary greatly. Some alters embody emotions that are split off; some serve functions like protecting, getting along in the world, controlling internal traffic; some handle traumatic, painful situations; some are destructive; some offer spiritual guidance. All alters and fragments carry memories.

In the middle range of the continuum, alters and fragments are aware of, and frequently communicate with, each other and with the host personality. This is termed co-consciousness. Farther along the continuum to the right, we find alters who have no awareness of each other. This amnesiac barrier can be between separate alters, and/or between alters (or alter layers) and host. When this happens, the host loses time—from minutes to years. By the time we reach the far right side of the arc, some, or all, of the alters are totally autonomous and may have different sets of clothes, wake up in cities far from home with no idea of how they got there; one alter may be a homebody with a husband and children, another a nun or priest, another a prostitute.

While giving presentations on multiplicity for professionals and multiples alike, the editors discovered that a need existed for a book comprised of stories by multiples who have worked through their multiplicity, and also through the integration process of becoming a singleton (our term). We reflected that such a book would have been extremely helpful to us while we were struggling through the pain and morass of remembering and then dealing with what we had remembered. How reassuring it would have been to have stories available of how others lived through the grief and horror of their backgrounds and, by so doing, blossomed.

We had several criteria and guidelines for our potential writers:

they be fully integrated, with one ego state operating the mind and body; they have a spiritual grounding; they be from diverse spiritual, geographic, and gender backgrounds.

This was our ideal. The reality, however, took us into new territory; we were not able to fulfill all our criteria. We learned that integration is truly an ongoing and sometimes fragile process. One can believe integration/fusion has been accomplished, only to find hidden layers and undiscovered alters. We believe ourselves fortunate to have had this truth revealed to us so clearly and honestly by our writers, and to have been witnesses to their courage and dedication to healing. We also learned that it is important not to place judgment on whether or not total integration has taken place, or, if it has taken place, whether or not it has "held" for six months or two years. Once again, we are reminded that it is the journey that is important, not the destination or conclusion—if a conclusion exists.

The eight stories included in *Multiple Journeys to One* give a picture of eight different modes of dissociating, eight different alter systems, eight different experiences of extreme child abuse, eight different processes of integration and fusion, and eight different forms of wholeness. Many of the backgrounds include incest, familial torture, Satanic Ritual Abuse, and programming. All include mental, emotional, physical, and spiritual abuse that happened at a young age.

We asked our writers to focus on their multiplicity and integration/fusion process rather than on in-depth descriptions of the abuse that led to their fragmentation. There are many books that recount the abuse of children, but few that are concerned with the physical, emotional, and spiritual process of multiplicity and integration.

In terms of multiplicity, wholeness can take many forms. For some, wholeness may mean co-consciousness between the alters and the host so that information is available to, and flows freely through, the total organism. For others, wholeness may signify integration, a state whereby the unit functions as one, while some, or all, of the alter system remains intact, able to function internally as identifiable ego states.

We are aware, from personal experience, from research, and from conversations with survivors and therapists, that integration, too, can be defined in various ways. Groups of alters can merge (come together) and have co-consciousness between other alter groups, but not with the host personality. An alter can choose to merge into another alter, or into the host's body while there are still separate alters. Sometimes a layer of alters merge, or integrate, so that the host personality thinks s/he is now one personality. Later, the therapist and host personality may find that a whole level of submerged alters exist under intense, layered programming. Fusion is what has commonly come to be termed integration: all of the alters permanently fuse into one personality, or ego state.

Neither of us suggests that integration (or fusion) is the only manner of healing. It is one path, the path explored by the women in this book. If other paths are taken, it speaks to our diversity; just as there is not one story—indeed, there are many stories—there is never just one right way to heal. In time, there will be stories exemplifying other paths. We look forward to reading them.

Not all the writers strove for integration; a few did not want to integrate and were, in fact, extremely fearful of the consequences: death of their alters; inability to cope with an unfamiliar world; loneliness. Integration happened spontaneously for the two of us. Some, like Margaret and Brooke, thought the process of integration was complete, only to discover more alters, or, like Carol, more alter layers. It is not unusual, however, when a newly integrated multiple is retraumatized, to find that the fusion has not taken place. In such situations, hidden alters, or layers of alters, surface. During the process of healing, it may happen that the multiple, believing that she is integrated, will not have the insight to be aware of her continuing multiplicity. We have learned that we cannot second-guess the wisdom of our inner selves; as long as we stay open to the possibilities of healing, however, our psyches will continue to reach for the Light. Jung believed that everything living strives for

wholeness. The problem, he said, is that "the right way to wholeness is made up, unfortunately, of fateful detours and wrong
turnings." It is not a straight path, but one that is snakelike, "a
path that unites the opposites ... and whose labyrinthine twists
and turns are not lacking in terrors."

You may wonder where the men are. It was not our intention to publish a book solely about female multiples. The fact is
that, with the exception of one man, we were unable to find
men willing to participate. Jonathan, by graciously contribut-
ing his drawings to our book, gifted us with a history that speaks
more eloquently than words. Will Riggan, in his article in the
Olympia Institute Quarterly, "The Shadow of Male Suffering," dis-
cusses the many reasons for this seeming absence of male survivors:

> For one example, males' easy access to anger, derived from cultural
> norms, serves as a useful block against the recognition of pain. Also,
> male relationships are far more regulated by power relations than
> are women's, and going into therapy is popularly understood as a
> sign of weakness, because it is a recognition of vulnerability (in too
> many minds those are synonymous). Related to that, men often hold
> their own sexual abuse as an intense stigma, a mark of feminization.
> Our culture reinforces both of those sorry conclusions: that to be
> abused is a stigma on the victim, and that feminization constitutes
> a reduction in status.

Four of the stories mention Satanic Ritual Abuse or SRA.
Some of the references may be difficult to accept; it is not
easy to read about any abuse visited on a defenseless child by
adults. These writers, however, have not imagined their abuse.
It happened. We offer a definition of Ritual Abuse from the
Ritual Abuse Task Force, Los Angeles County Commission for
Women, because we feel it important to provide a context for
some of the stories you are about to read.

> Ritual abuse is a brutal form of abuse of children, adolescents, and
> adults, consisting of physical, sexual, and psychological abuse, and
> involving the use of rituals. Ritual does not necessarily mean sa-
> tanic. However, most survivors state that they were ritually abused
> as part of satanic worship for the purpose of indoctrinating them

into satanic beliefs and practices. Ritual abuse rarely consists of a single episode. It usually involves repeated abuse over an extended period of time.

DID does not arise from just a few terrifying experiences. It is the mind's way of coping brilliantly with repeated abuse that would otherwise be intolerable to the psyche of a child before the age of five. Lest the reader think the abuses mentioned in this book are beyond belief, let us set the record straight. People we have talked to in law enforcement tell us that in states across the country, there is evidence that crimes are committed by self-styled Satanists and by Satanic cults. This evidence is frequently not submitted in court, although testimony often clearly indicates the ritualistic nature of the crimes. Attorneys hesitate to prosecute a case that deals with SRA, we have been told, instead, charging lesser offenses. Many jurors—like the population as a whole—cannot admit that such dark things happen. There are, however, documented cases of SRA that have been tried and won.

There have also been a number of court cases, including day care centers, in which convictions have been obtained, only to have the verdicts overturned on minor technicalities. Frequently, prosecutors drop charges in order to spare children the ordeal of having to testify again.

Whether we like it or not, our fellow human beings are, indeed, capable of this type of depravity.

There is also reference to government/military abuse. With the release of documents under the Freedom of Information Act, the Presidential Advisory Committee on Human Radiation Experiments (1995), and the Advocacy Committee for Human Experimentation Survivors–Mind Control (ACHES-MC), we felt it important to mention and be open to all possibilities of covert abuse and its consequences. Those interested in further information might investigate *Search for the Manchurian Candidate: The CIA and Mind Control, Secret History of the Behavioral Sciences,* by John Marks, 1979, and/or *Operation Mind Control,* by Walter Bowart, 1994.

Although you will note many commonalities in these stories, they are striking in their dissimilarities. Ages vary from thirty to seventy. Many of our writers grew up along the West Coast, but several were from the central states and the East Coast. Religious/belief backgrounds include Protestant, Catholic, Jewish, atheist, and more than a few Mormons. Some of us come from multigenerational cult families; some from families that were not cult-involved but that perpetrated incest and then turned a blind eye to its devastating results; some from families that included both cult abuse and incest.

The writers identify with differing areas along the dissociation continuum: co-consciousness; co-consciousness with time losses; amnesiac barriers between some, but not all, alters, resulting in more frequent and longer time losses; amnesiac barriers between most, or all alters, accompanied by large time gaps.

In addition to the above differences, our writers come from different perspectives in their integration processes. Some dealt with difficult memories through their alters, dreams, and body memories, then integrated. A few had limited memories and are just recently starting to remember more. For still others, new levels of abuse surfaced after integration.

We have made no attempt to cover the totality of experiences involving abuse, multiplicity, and integration/fusion. We trust that somewhere within our eight stories, the reader will find the connection that will lead to hope, strength, insight, inspiration, and a unifying spirituality.

Some of the writers have used fictitious names for the protection of themselves and their families, and for legal reasons. Perhaps, as those of us who have been abused find the words and the courage to speak of our experiences, there will be more positive public awareness, and consequently more safety.

We have learned that integration/fusion does not stop when all alter personalities have been gathered under one roof. That is just the first step. The second step is integrating the integration. This can be a difficult, confusing, exciting, tumultuous time. How does one function in this new world? How does one consciousness survive the onslaught of memories, feelings, sensations without splitting or delegating responsibility to alters who, in the past, apportioned out the pain and confusion so that it was manageable? This is a time to treat oneself with gentleness, love, and compassion. It is a time to draw upon one's resources: trusted friends for support, therapists or counselors for guidance, oneself for forgiveness and spiritual sustenance.

We want to add a cautionary note here to multiples and therapists alike. In addition to its amazing rewards, integrating the integration carries with it its own set of challenges, as mentioned above. This is not a time to interrupt therapy. To reach this exciting, intense phase of a lengthy recovery and then choose to stop therapy, or be forced out on one's own, tends to duplicate the original trauma. If problems arise, please consider using ingenuity, creativity, and consideration to work them out. But do work them out.

The passage we eight women have made from multiplicity to varying stages of wholeness is a testament to our resilience, persistence, courage, and spirit. We, the editors, are grateful for the patience and cooperation of our writers. They have endured, with grace and good humor, the usual, seemingly endless annoying edits and rewrites. Both of us have come to feel a closeness, a camaraderie, and a special bonding with these remarkable human beings. Our book has been pivotal in healing us all. Our experiences have deepened our belief that integration is a process of love and acceptance.

Brooke

I am a wombin[1] on a spiritual journey of personal growth based on respect for the earth and all life. As a way to use my life experiences to offer compassionate support to others, I am currently working on a Masters Degree in Psychology. Intuition and sensitivity, though born out of adversity, are gifts I have to offer now. A sense of humor and playfulness are very important to my healing and enjoyment of life.

BACKGROUND. By September of 1989 I learned that incest with my dad started when I was about three months old, and lasted on a regular basis until I was five years old. He was a very sadistic man and sexually abused everyone in my family, including my mom. The incest slowed down when we moved into a new home when I was five, but never really stopped until I moved out of the house at age eighteen.

My father also involved me in pornography and ritual abuse. I was around two years old when these occurred. The pornography "studio" was set up in someone's home where different pornographic scenes were photographed and filmed. Many children, including myself and my siblings, were drugged so that we would perform better in front of the cameras. Both the porn and ritual abuse lasted until the age of six and then re-emerged briefly when I was a teenager.

---

[1] *Wombin*: in order to have a naming and identification completely my own, that has no connection to *man* or *male* as in *woman* or *female*, I have chosen to use this spelling. For further reading on this subject I recommend Louise Goueffic's book, *Breaking the Patriarchal Code*.

PRE-MERGING. While I was still doing my undergraduate work, a Four-Year-Old part of myself was beginning to emerge. At the time, I didn't recognize her as being separate from me; I just thought I was coming from a young space. I recall riding my bicycle and the Four-Year-Old part would label things as I was riding: tree, house, car, bird—simple things. I remember speaking of this "odd behavior" to Marge, the therapist I was seeing at college. I didn't have a clue what was happening to me, and Marge could only listen. During other sessions some part of me could barely get the words out, at times almost stuttering. During my work with her, I had my first incest memory. I remembered being molested by two different cousins. It became obvious to her that I needed long term therapy, and more support than she would be able to give me. She did a beautiful job of helping me with the transition of finding another counselor who could better meet my needs. I am incredibly thankful to her.

A few months into being comfortable with my new therapist, more sexual abuse memories began to surface. I had been working full time at a highly stressful job in a residential treatment center for boys who were labeled severely emotionally disturbed. Some of the boys had been taken from their homes due to emotional, physical, and sexual abuse. Seeing them deal with their own horrid pasts was triggering me. The longer I worked with the kids, the harder it got. A pressure was building inside me.

I was already attending Survivors of Incest Anonymous (SIA) meetings (for the abuse that occurred with my cousins), but the thought of consciously acknowledging that I was an incest survivor scared me. It was easier for me to think the abuse with my cousins happened in isolated incidents, than to accept the fact that the sexual abuse had occurred continuously in my own home with my father, whom I thought I could trust.

While attending SIA meetings, I was introduced to the concept of the inner child and multiple personalities. There I met, and became friends with, a woman who spoke about and nurtured these child parts of herself. She role-modeled for me how she honored each of her kids at their own developmental stages.

She saw clearly that I was in trouble in my job and in my life, and she asked me to talk to my therapist about my feelings of hopelessness. I did to a tiny degree, but I did not reveal the fact that I was actively suicidal.

In March of 1989, I hit an emotional bottom and attempted suicide. When I survived it, I became willing to face the issues I had been attempting to run from. I finally had the courage to acknowledge that my father was my perpetrator. Then I was able to hear my Four-Year-Old talking to my therapist, which was something I had never witnessed. My Four-Year-Old held the key to my intuition and helped me see the bigger picture of what was happening to me emotionally. I finally "got it" that she was somewhat separate from me. It was mind boggling. I heard her voice talking to me on a regular basis.

The Four-Year-Old talked to my therapist about the sexual abuse, and the memories that now wanted recognition. As the Four (as she referred to herself) began to feel safer and stronger in my body, more inner children emerged, along with much chaos. Everyone wanted time in my body; they were acting out, they were scared, and I wasn't taking care of them. I felt suicidal often and ended up on antidepressants.

My counselor helped me realize I have a dissociative disorder, similar to multiple personalities, and encouraged me to take responsibility for these inner children, and provide for their containment. My actual diagnosis is Dissociative Disorder, not otherwise specified. Unlike those with multiple personalities, I miraculously managed to keep my core sense of identity and have been conscious of my inner children as they emerge. As I have retrieved my memories, these inner children have shown up to talk about what happened to them. Dealing with the memories had a domino effect. For example, my Four-Year-Old would have a memory and could only share a portion of it; then another inner child would return to help finish that particular memory. This pattern continued for quite some time as I continually processed memories and met more inner children. In time, and with nurturing support, I have consciously merged many of my fragmented parts.

Brooke

13

The process of merging was one of necessity. I was the only adult in my body with twenty-five kids all under the age of seven! I had read Frank Putnam's book, *Diagnosis and Treatment of Multiple Personality Disorder,* and realized that I could merge/blend together several kids who were similar in age. This process was a group decision and all the children involved had to be in agreement for the merging to happen.

In one such incident, I went into a trancelike state (like I normally do to talk with my kids), and had around me at least eight of the five-year-olds. I explained that those who wanted to, could merge and still be with me. Most of them had already worked through their portion of the memories and had also had the opportunity to be playful, rambunctious kids. I made it clear to them that there was no pressure to merge, that this was something they could decide individually. Some chose to, yet a few wanted to remain separate.

When they merged with me, I felt their energies mingling with my core self. It reminded me of the sparkly energy I used to see on the television show *Star Trek* when people were "beamed" to their desired location. I knew if it wasn't right for the kids to merge, it would be like repelling magnets.

In 1990, after reading Vicki Noble's book, *Shakti Woman,* I intuitively knew I needed to work with a shaman to help me on my journey. Within two weeks, I met a medicine woman named Leslie who changed my life. She is a radical feminist who has been in practice for over twenty years. Leslie sees people individually and in groups, and facilitates conferences that help wombin find their voice and learn to love themselves. I was scared to meet her, but knew intuitively she would be safe.

Leslie taught me about negative entities, an energy form that doesn't have my higher interest in mind. Having an entity in my body is like having a cloud hanging over me and standing in its shadow. I became so used to its being there that I didn't know it had been there until it was removed. For example, I used to think that I (or one of my kids) felt suicidal, but this wasn't the case some of the time. It was the entity not wanting me to discover the severity of the memories. The more fear my body felt, the more the entity took over. Leslie helped me become aware of when an entity was trying to inhabit my body, and what to do to release it.

Prior to merging my last six kids, I interviewed Leslie to ask her about her experience of my coming more into my adult body.

Leslie: Your adult was terrified when she first came to see me. She was suffering from the wounds of her childhood. There was enough of the adult to find healing, but the adult's presence would come in and out. The adult wasn't used to being in the body.

Brooke: So what was your focus with us in the beginning?

Leslie: It seems that in the beginning I was helping to uncover buried pictures that related to the trauma. I would talk about some of the things I saw that were deep in the layers of the subconscious[2] and unconscious[3], and also loved you the best way I knew how.

Brooke: How would you describe removing all those negative entities that were around us?

Leslie: Entities seem to have a variety of forms. They are beings who are not in body, and vary from being helpful (like Spirit Guides), to inhabiting space that doesn't belong to them. They are attracted to one person through powerful emotions such as anger or fear. The latter kind of entities are invasive, take up space, and possess the body they are attracted to. They can cause havoc to the host, and the host can be in various states of turmoil, such as confusion and depression. What is interesting about entities is that the host can be in therapy, but the entity

[2]*Subconscious:* occurring without conscious perception, or with only slight perception, on the part of the individual. (Webster, *New World Dictionary,* NY. 1988 Third Edition)

[3]*Unconscious:* the sum of all thoughts, memories, impulses, desires, feelings etc. of which the individual is not conscious but which influences the emotions and behaviors. (*Ibid.*)

isn't. So, sometimes there's a feeling of being stuck; the host is trying to heal, yet is feeling despair about the work. That can come from an entity attachment because the entities aren't working on themselves.

Brooke: We had entities who were connected to family members. It took working with you to differentiate what was mine and what was someone else's.

Leslie: The more one loves oneself, the more one can distinguish who is self and who is other.

Brooke: You first gave us an animal totem to help us empower ourselves to get in our body more. That is when you introduced us to our white horse.

Leslie: The reason for doing animal totem work is because it helps ground the person in a nonintellectual way. It grounds the body. It grounds the Spirit and connects one with a healing source that is in the realm of the Spirit Animals. In a shamanic view, we all have animal totems. Most of us in western cultures don't know that, and therefore we don't know who our totems are. Shamans say there is much suffering that results from not being connected with one's totem. Having an animal totem means being connected through the Mother. That is a very significant definition. So there is something about connecting with the energy of a totem or power animal that accesses healing energy that isn't measurable by scientific standards, but it is very strong medicine.

Brooke: Having the totems helped me feel safer in the world, but I had to remember to call on them.

Leslie: That's right. It is an active relationship. The shamanic people say that when you're not in connection with your power animal or totem, they go away. You are then susceptible to illness or loss of power. Restoring power is very important in any kind of healing work.

When a being (not just a multiple) recognizes his/her Oneness, in all ways, there is a strong sense of oneness. Nobody goes away. There is a profound feeling of being one, not fragmented. There is no true separation. There is a celebration of Oneness.

Four-Year-Old: If we go, will the adult still have an inner kid?

Leslie: Yes. The adult is the mother, maiden, and crone.

Four-Year-Old: So, that's what the adult is going to grow up to be?

Leslie: Right.

Four-Year-Old: But the adult says she wants to keep some of my energy—my essence—around.

Leslie: She will.

Four-Year-Old: What about the spunky teenager? She helped reclaim anger for the adult.

Leslie: She will keep that spunkiness. It's just that you will all be together rather than scattered about. You'll be experiencing being all together in one place. Before, there was a circle, and some of you were inside the circle and some of you were outside the circle. The people outside the circle felt separated and were afraid. They felt cut off and were not happy. Now that everyone is inside the circle, it is like you can dance together.

Four-Year-Old: The Fourteen and Fifteen-Year-Olds are still outside the circle.

Leslie: But they are much closer to the edge. I'm seeing them included in the circle.

Four-Year-Old: What about Rising Sun? We know she's no longer a baby. We think she's around fifteen now and is slowly merging into the adult. Rising Sun holds the memory of never being hurt. We kids who are still here are afraid that when Rising Sun gets to be the adult's age, we are all going to be integrated. Is that true?

Leslie: Yes, it looks like that from here. This is the direction you're headed.

Brooke: Early on, you started doing Soul Retrievals with us. Then you taught me how to do it for myself with the help of my Spirit Guides.

Leslie: There was already much you were doing when you weren't in session here. You already had a psychic attunement and you felt at home in those realms.

Brooke: Can you explain what a soul retrieval is?

Leslie: Soul Retrieval is a shamanic practice, another way of restoring power, like a power animal retrieval. The Soul Retrieval revolves around finding one's lost parts and bringing them back into the body. It's not like dissociation because these parts are actually parts of the Soul, the Essence, the energy that was lost. For the Being/the Host to survive, behavior is often created which manifests forms for holding whatever needs to be protected. So, retrieving lost parts of one's essence means that something was lost during a trauma. Trauma has to do with soul loss which can deplete a person's power, their sense of well being and the energy they have available to heal. Sometimes one gets sick due to soul loss, so it involves the shaman–actually the shamama, as I like to say–acting as intermediary between the Spirit Realms and the Earth Realms. Finding those lost parts and putting them back into the person's body is basically what a Soul Retrieval is.

Brooke: In the beginning, doing the soul retrievals was very intense.

Leslie: Well, it is intense because what is returned is a part that was split off because of the pain. So when the lost souls return they bring back memories and feelings of that time period. And having a Soul Retrieval can bring about much change.

Brooke: Yes. I'm finding that as the integration process continues, I have more room in the body.

Leslie: Well, you have more room in the body because you have had those entities removed (depossessions). And, also, the other personalities take up space. So as they come back into Oneness, there's going to be the feeling of more room because they aren't going to be drawing you to the outside of the circle to their existence. When they come in, and there's a sense of merging, this creation of Oneness is also one of spaciousness.

Brooke: I've been so used to dealing with their chaos outside the circle, that it's hard for me to get used to this calmness, Leslie.

Leslie: You will. It's just not what you've been used to.

Beyond learning to do the soul retrievals and entity removals by myself, Leslie taught me how to connect with my own Spirit Guides. The guides have my highest good in mind to assist me on my path. My guides—Hecate, White Buffalo Calf Woman, and Quan Yin—are separate from my body; they show up when I do my trance work. They will walk over to me, or I call to them, and we talk. They are invaluable in retrieving my inner kids. When it's timely, they also assist in merging the kids. For instance, while in trance, Hecate may approach me on her black horse and tell me there is a child of mine who is ready to come back. Together we retrieve that part of me. White Buffalo Calf Woman then assists by removing any negative entities from that child and comforts her until I have time to process this, either on my own or in therapy.

MERGING PROCESS. The following is an example of my journaling as I was going through the process of integrating.

11/24/96, SUNDAY, 2 P.M.
   I check in with the kids and ask the Four-Year-Old, "Are you going

to be leaving soon?"

She says, "Yes. Rising Sun, now fifteen, says it is time for me to merge into you. I don't want to go." Tears. "Rising Sun says I'll still be in you."

I'm frustrated. WHY CAN'T THIS WAIT! *I knew kids were going to be merging into me, but I thought the Four-Year-Old and I would always be around.*

Then, addressing the Four-Year-Old, I say, "You've been here the longest. You're the one who helps me be in my feelings and is so intuitive. I don't want you to go. I thought you would always be with me."

I decide to check in with Rising Sun to see what is happening. She answers, "She'll still be in you, but it is time for you to be in your adult body more. You've relied on the Four, which has been helpful; now it's time for you to rely on your own inner strength. The Four is you. You're very intuitive and have that playful spirit as well."

I'm feeling really sad. I don't want this to happen, but I don't think I have much control over it. This integration is happening naturally and I need to trust that this is for my highest good.

11/26/96, 10:30 P.M.

Don't want to sleep. Am anxious that I'll wake up and the Four-Year-Old will be gone. So many changes! She's going over our entire life, cleaning things up from the past, and saying good-bye to people she has been close with. I've been crying every day.

12/2/96, MONDAY, 6:30 P.M.

The Four is merging into me as I'm writing. When I awoke this morning, she said it was time for her to leave, but I wanted her to wait until I was home from school. When I returned home, the Four-Year-Old called two friends and said good-bye to them, that she would still be around but in a different form.

This is what I'm feeling from the Four-Year-Old: "I'm still around, kind of. Rising Sun is having me slowly merge into your adult body. I am also gathering all the bad stuff that happened to us and am doing a collective soul retrieval. I know all this inner work is making you tired, but I like being older now. I haven't fully merged into you yet. Like I said, I am gathering up the ones who haven't returned and this will take some time. If you want to know about how old I am now, I'd say around eleven or twelve. But I am in your body. That is why you still can hear from me, but can no longer see my head. Pretty weird, huh?!"

Developmentally, the Four-Year-Old and Rising Sun needed to grow up before they could fully merge into me. I relied so much on both of them, but primarily on the Four-Year-Old; she was the intuitive one and the person who could be in feelings.

12/8/96, SUNDAY AFTERNOON

One of my greatest fears of merging is that I won't have my inner kids to validate my memories of abuse. From my head I know this isn't so, but internally I am confused and I need time to sit with these changes. Rising Sun is now twenty-one.

The Four-Year-Old is now around eighteen. I can still hear her voice some, but it's obvious she is older. But also, I think I have in me the voice she had when she was four.

Four-Year-Old: "Hey, adult —I'm just older now. I'm in your body now. Things are going to be okay."

1/7/97 TUESDAY, 6 P.M.

On December 21st—the Solstice—Rising Sun and my two teenagers (Hummingbird and Wolf) merged into me. I knew this was going to happen with Rising Sun, but it wasn't until several days after a sweat that I realized the teenagers were also integrated inside me. I went into shock and called on my Spirit Guides who had been with me at the sweat. [A sweat lodge is a cross cultural ceremony of purification of the body, mind and spirit. This purification is something I have done every few months to help ground me and release any emotions. I have always used the lodge for a healing for my highest good, and for my inner kids. This particular day, my Spirit Guides did the healing work on my teenagers while I participated in this ceremony.] I felt the energy shifting inside me, but wasn't aware fully of what was happening.

All I have left is the Eleven-Year-Old. It is so quiet on the inside—I don't know how to be with it.

I feel so vulnerable in the world right now. I have increased my therapy to twice weekly (having previously dropped it to once a week) to help me through this transition, and to look at this process while in a trance state. Two major things are happening in my life right now. The first is that I am going through my life from birth and am releasing all that happened. It is like a VCR constantly running tapes of my life, going over any major traumas that still need to be looked at. Currently I am up to age six. On Monday's session I brought another Six-Year-Old back. She didn't even need to tell her story, just have the experience of being safe in the body today. I could feel her talking in me, and I was consciously aware when she was in my body. The second transition is remembering, on a body level, what it was like when I split off into other parts. It felt like my head had this big horizontal crack in it and I was falling into a bottomless hole in complete terror. When I integrated, I re-experienced the horror of splitting into my fragmented parts.

During the merging process, I was constantly in abreactions[4], and easily triggered by many people, places, and things. It was a scary time for me. My childhood abuse was ruling my life, and I was immersed in it. I was drowning in the past and couldn't see who I was as an adult. I was allowing my kids to run my body because I didn't want to feel all that was coming up with the memories. There were times when I would ignore their pain because I didn't want to feel the sadness in myself. At the same time, though, I chose friends in my life who kept me immersed in the process. All my friends were incest, pornography, and/ or ritual abuse survivors and discussions of our abuse, therapy, and our inner kids was a major part of our connection. When I look back on this, I realize I found a safe group of people to connect with, but also cut myself off from the beauty of each day. I remained caught up in the past, and wasn't creating enough of a life for myself in the present.

When I merged all of my inner children, except for my Eleven-Year-Old who still needs time to grow, I felt lost being in the world. I was used to hearing the voices of my inner kids,

---

[4]*Abreaction*: emotional release or discharge after recalling a painful experience that has been repressed because it was consciously intolerable. (American Psychiatric Association, 1980, p. 1).

getting caught up in their weekly dramas, and experiencing the chaos I'd grown accustomed to. I was scared the first two weeks after the integration; since then, I've continued working on how to be an integrated adult in my body.

Now I feel safer being in the present, being in my body. I have the energy to expand my world and the people I connect with. I feel fuller today: I take up more space in my body. Colors seem brighter. It is like a cloud has lifted, and my eyes are now open to see the world more clearly. I still feel vulnerable. I don't know exactly how to "do life." I don't know how to be with all the feelings that different parts of me once held. I am still working on feeling joy.

In the past, adults were perpetrators and I never wanted to be an adult or a perpetrator. The fact that my eyes are open clears the way for me to observe healthy role models as I learn how to be an open hearted and grounded wombin. My therapist and the friends in my life today have the willingness and courage to keep working on themselves and to speak their truth. This enables me to begin honoring the feminine aspects of myself, which in the past I had been too fearful to express. The feminine, for me, means learning to feel comfortable in my body, opening up to Spirit, surrendering, and allowing my intuition to come forth.

What I have discovered is that I like who I am today. I don't need the chaos I had in my childhood, or what I had when my inner kids started coming back to me in 1990. It is now quiet in my head; outside sounds are clearer because I have more room to listen. And yet, I am incredibly grateful to my inner kids. They saved my life and I will always love them. Fragmenting into thirty plus parts was a creative way to deal with the horrendous abuse I grew up with.

I sometimes miss my fragmented inner kids, but their qualities are still within me. As an adult, I'd always felt the grief of not having a life of my own. Today I have my life back. I am still getting memories, but they aren't running the show now. I like having things quieter on the inside.

It is now March 1997 and in the past month a few inner kids

have been retrieved during memories, but they immediately integrated into me. I feel the process of integration is ongoing for all of us who choose to be on our healing path. In the counseling and crisis related work I do to help other people with their healing, I have seen how many of us have lost parts of ourselves and have been wounded in some way. I think we all have aspects of ourselves we need to reclaim, regardless of the diagnosis.

MAY, 1997

In the past few months, I have discovered another layer of memories I had never known before. Since getting these memories, more fragmented parts have returned, but they are only around for a short time. I need to be with each part just long enough to process the memory, then that part merges into me. This can happen as quickly as an hour; the longest any one part has stayed has been two weeks. I'm aware this process of finding new inner kids may go on for awhile. This is okay, because it's much easier on me today since I am conscious of what's happening.

M emories don't affect me like they did in the past. My life no longer stops because I have an abuse memory to process. What is still an issue is my level of dissociation when I am home alone: I go from one activity to another without being fully aware of what I am doing. Since I am used to living out of body, having all this extra space around me takes getting used to. I feel that as I learn to honor my wide range of feelings more I won't need to dissociate as much.

I still do trance work by myself and during therapy, not only to process memory work, but to hear what my Spirit Guides are saying to me. Part of my healing has been to learn to stay present in this realm, fully in body.

R ELATIONSHIPS. In the seven years I have been doing memory work, I have been in two romantic relationships. The first relationship lasted only six months. We were both in the throes of memories and both dissociative. We couldn't communicate because neither of us knew how to speak our truth.

Recently, I was involved with a wombin for thirteen months. It was a "safe" relationship in that she supported me in speaking my truth. However, she could not be emotionally present for me. In this way I stayed safe. Breaking up with Annie was incredibly painful, but I need connections in my life that will enable me to continue to grow.

Meeting new people is hard for me. I feel like I'm a Vietnam War vet and am not sure how much of my history to disclose, how to share or what not to share (especially now that I'm in a Master's Program). How do you say to someone that you've been in a war, but it was a war that society does not acknowledge? This is something I am trying to work out.

Given all this, the focus in my weekly therapy sessions continues to be learning to stay present. With my therapist and friends, I am learning how to grapple with a wide range of feelings. For example, when anger comes up, I express it appropriately by talking about it. If the anger lingers, I give it physical expression, such as walking or running, to release the adrenaline. When my kids were present, my Fifteen-Year-Old was primarily the one who held the anger and would express it by causing confusion and pain; the result was that my core self would withdraw from all the inner turmoil. Although I have found other ways to experience my emotions, sometimes it's still scary for me to feel them.

F ORGIVENESS. Forgiveness is still a hard issue for me. I look at forgiveness as a gradual process. For so long, my inner children blamed themselves for the abuse, feeling that by doing so they would gain control over a situation. Total forgiveness hasn't arrived, since I find that I occasionally push myself more than I need to. Rather than giving myself a break, I'll add another stressful situation, just like my perpetrators did to me. For example, I spoke with my doctor about going off thyroid medication (she agreed), but I chose to quit the drug during school finals. The timing was a poor choice! If I had forgiven myself, I wouldn't have brought this extra stress into my life—I'd have had more self-compassion.

There is still a part of me that wants my mother to be different than she really is, to be the mom I always wanted her to be. Although she was not one of my perpetrators, she was forced to participate in the abuse. In my kid feelings, I still wish my mom had been an assertive adult and had taken me out of danger. As a child, I wanted to take care of her, to protect her from the abuse. I've needed to look at the depths of the enmeshment and learn not to take care of her feelings. She's not a multiple, but clearly dissociates frequently. I am beginning to forgive her; I have compassion for her and what she went through to keep the family intact in the midst of a constant nightmare. I am learning, on a deeper level, that I am in charge of my life, that I can take care of myself, and that I am separate from my mother.

In these past seven years, I have been able to see how different my mom and I are. Her self-esteem is based on material objects–having new clothes, the right car, getting her nails and hair done, having the "perfect house"–while my sense of self is more connected with the Earth and maintaining my spirituality. My lifelong commitment is to grow, to value integrity, to pursue my goals and to share my life with my family of friends. My mom and I live in two different worlds. Because of this realization I have been able to say, "I love you mom, but I need to live my life. I'm not going to pretend that things are okay. I'm not going to live in a fantasy world that you've created where you believe your husband would never do those things! I'm no longer going to be part of the lie."

I no longer feel as much anger toward my father. In the process of recovering my memories, I filed two police reports on him, went through Victim Witness, and tried joint therapy. I miss having a "Dad," but he was never a real father. In our therapy together, he was never willing to acknowledge the sexual abuse and, given that, I chose to tell him that I would not have any contact with him. After several years of not seeing my dad, intuitively I felt I should go and see my "family" at Christmas time. Prior to going, I took care of myself and my inner kids by making it clear to my dad that he couldn't touch me or take any pictures of me while I was there. I was nervous about seeing him, but psychically I looked him in the eyes and said, "I am not afraid of you anymore and I do remember what happened." Three days after I left, my dad died of heart failure. I was glad I had had the opportunity to see him. This last visit showed me how far I had come in establishing boundaries. With his death, I now feel safer in the world.

Even though I still have memories, I work on them by releasing the anger from my body in healthy ways. In doing trance work, I have spoken to my dad numerous times and have been able to direct my anger towards him. It has taken years of working with him in the trance world for him to acknowledge what he did. Since then, I have felt calmer.

In September of 1997, I had a bicycle accident and ended up with seven cervical fractures, two broken ribs, a partially dislocated shoulder, and temporary loss of a full range of motion in my left arm. I was hospitalized for eighteen days. For four months I wore a neck brace, did exercises prescribed by my physical therapist, and relearned how to use my left arm. I received Jin Shin Jyutsu®[5] treatments up to six times a week to help stop the daily muscle spasms. All the therapies I received helped me come into my body in a new way. I am still learning what this means. Not having been fully connected to my feelings and my body led to this serious accident.

I have been through many transformations since then. A new level of abuse memories surfaced and new inner kids emerged. Most merged into me, but currently I still have a few kids. The biggest change is that I don't have to live my life from a place of fear. The abuse is really over now and, even though the new memories are intense, I don't feel swallowed up by them.

This accident was, and continues to be, a turning point in my life. From necessity, I had the opportunity to let go of control. I couldn't take care of myself: I needed help from the hospital staff and my friends to support me. In the past, I had held on tightly in order to take care of my own needs and now I was

[5]Ancient, hands-on healing art of energy balance and harmony.

being asked to surrender completely and be present in my body. However, as a result of talking with my guides, Quan Yin and White Buffalo Calf Woman, I have learned how to surrender. Leslie did a soul retrieval at the moment of the accident. This part immediately merged into my body and in trance I saw how my guides were there during the accident; they held my neck so it wasn't broken completely. The doctors were amazed that I could still walk and that I wasn't paralyzed from this injury.

Most important, I have seen that this accident (perhaps not an accident) has allowed me to feel, and accept the love of my friends. As I learned how to accept who I was, and how to open my heart and receive warmth, my inner children became free to merge into me.

As I continued to heal from the accident, I felt integration coming. One Saturday in February 1998, I went for a walk, sat by a creek, closed my eyes, and went into trance. I could see all my inner kids sitting in a circle, along with my Spirit Guide, White Buffalo Calf Woman. She held our sacred pipe, for which I gave thanks. I smoked, but didn't inhale. I then went to my children saying what I had learned from each of them. As I went around the circle, each one blended into my energy. As the last merged, I cried and gave thanks. As far as I know, after five months into the healing of my fractures, all my inner kids have merged into me.

Maybe I have integrated. Time will tell if I am ready to have those feelings merge directly into me. Though I sense that new children will come back, this is not important. I trust my process. Whatever happens, I know I will take responsibility for my life. In the meantime, I continue in therapy and will do any healing modality that will further my growth. I am learning to be in the stillness without hearing my inner children's voices. I am also making time daily to stay in touch with my feelings. This process has been a blessing in learning how to love myself. I know now that this entire process is just the beginning.

Margaret

My life now is full and joyful. I have four wonderfully happy and well-adjusted boys, ages seventeen to seven, who keep me stretched to my limits and yet sustain me. I am about to graduate from Antioch University with a liberal arts/psychology degree. I hope to complete an MSW degree. I have a toolbox full of methodologies, including Rapid Eye Technology[1], which I put to use in my private practice as I serve others who are still "broken." I hope to help my clients recognize the fact that everyone is whole and complete at their core, and claim that part of themselves, as I have.

I remember the day it all came to a head—the day I knew I needed help. I had been injured, bedridden for ten weeks with a herniated disk; in addition, I suffered increasingly difficult cycles of premenstrual stress (PMS). I had four sons, ranging in ages from one to eleven. One evening, as I rushed to a meeting, I picked up all the kids' stuff to get out the door, turned off the lights, put the cat out, and hobbled to the van. When I got into the car, I turned to my four precious sons and screamed, "YOU LITTLE BASTARDS." I bawled them out for just waiting peacefully for me in the car while I did all the getting ready. It was then I knew—I don't call my children names. This isn't the person I wanted to be, let alone the mother I wanted for my sons.

I went to my gynecologist, complaining of PMS. He assured me that I had major depression, not just PMS and referred me

[1] *Rapid Eye Technology*: can help release the charge from conscious or unconscious memories and conditioning without the need to reexperience or remember trauma or conditioning in its original intensity.

to a psychiatrist.

I was eventually hospitalized for my depression, during which time I saw a newly trained clinical hypnotherapist. While in treatment with her, I discovered the first of the memories. In addition to my older brother's sexual abuse, I remembered my father's alcoholism, the brutal physical abuse by my entire family, and much more. Under hypnosis, I had abreactions that graphically detailed sexual abuse beginning at birth, or shortly thereafter. Scraps of memories returned to testify to sadistic abuse. My subconscious mind and body remembered my father's sexual abuse of me beginning when I was born, wherein he would put his mouth on my vagina and breasts. I cut my baby teeth on my father's penis; he played "horsey," with me bouncing on his lap astride his erect penis. By the time I was two, he had taught me not to cry when he or his friends/customers used me as their sexual plaything. Unfortunately, my inexperienced therapist didn't know what to do with me, and on many occasions I left her office feeling wounded.

Depression became my constant companion. I spent most of my time in the fetal position in my bed. "Tell me before you call 911," I'd tell my children, "but otherwise, leave me alone." I finally sought the help of a therapist who was recommended as a specialist in childhood abuse and incest. Actually, she dealt more in marriage counseling. She and my husband insisted on working on our marriage. I insisted that I needed to work on my own issues, and that I was not up to the "emotional algebra" of marriage counseling. Neither of them heard me, and the upshot was that my husband divorced me, leaving me with no income, no insurance, no home, no support of any kind–physical or emotional. He kept the children and made me leave our home. I was so debilitated that I felt it would be better for my children if I left and allowed someone else to take care of them. My husband and I saw a mediator, who wrote up the divorce according to our agreement. (It was only after I left him and was free of his constant verbal and emotional abuse, that I was able to heal to the point where I could have the children returned to me. It was then, too, that I was able to see the folly of my previous thinking, and sue him for joint custody and child support. He never made up for the time he had left me destitute.)

At the time, I was devastated. I didn't know what to do. I was able to turn to my Church, which provided me with rent and groceries. I asked my therapist to help me with my personal issues now that she had succeeded in finishing off my marriage. Her response was, "Oh, I don't have the expertise to help you. Your case is way too difficult for me—I couldn't keep you safe." Needless to say, I was FURIOUS! Why hadn't she told me that eighteen months earlier? She did give me a referral, however.

Before this therapist referred me, she had been really proud to be able to diagnose my Obsessive Compulsive Disorder (OCD), although she told me that no one knows how OCD is developed. I knew, and wrote this poem to illustrate my knowing.

Porcelain Bisque

I've come to see myself
once lovely porcelain
now cracked, rebroken cracked again,
and countless times reglued.
and painted—over and over and over and over
and over and over and over and over.
I feel as though I used to be
a sugar bowl of bisque
Fragile, flawless, exquisite.

And then, the men,
the ten or more
who played their evil games.

Oblivious to my tenderness,
Ignorant of my worth
They all reached forth with grasping thumb,
to break away a piece of me.

I rescued every single piece
and glued it back in place.
and carefully painted every seam, over and over and over
and over and over and over and over and over

Margaret

To cover them, I counted
lines upon the highway
every step to school
poles and scalloped wires.

I honed my intellect
adding numbers all day long
and multiplying, too,
tracing every letter
spelling every word
typing, typing, typing,
or shorthand curlicues.

All inside my head, of course.
For no one ever knew
that every breath was measured
every step was counted,
and every line defined.

I rode my bike in China (as a missionary)
for sixty hours a week.
And every moment diligent
to aim the front wheel right
I halved the painted shoulder line
on every single street.

And as I halved, I counted
in Chinese – over and over and over and over and over
and over and over and over and over and over and over

Before I had my Doublemint
to help replace the thumb,
there was cotton wool or mattress tick,
with which I filled the emptiness
and served to keep me dumb.

And don't forget the warm spot (inside my elbow)
With the three-sided vein.
that I fondled with a fingertip
as I typed or spelled or counted
in cadence taps of three, over and over and over and over and over
and over and over and over and over and over and over and over

Did I mention I sing, as well?
Yes, little nursery rhymes
or on a good day, even hymns
but only one refrain, over and over and over and over and over
and over and over and over and over and over and over and over.

Thus I painted over the cracks
The only means of knowing
That I had been destroyed.

I functioned very well,
as anyone could see.
I was quite amazing
so talented and smart.

No one would ever guess
Least of all, myself.
I birthed my babies, one to four
and carried in my bowl
the sugar for them all.

And as the years have taken
their unrelenting toll
The glue has started peeling,
beneath the coats of paint.

I gave them all my sweetness
and they scraped the sides for more,
But since no one ever filled me,
There wasn't any more.

As they've continued scraping,
the cracks have come to show
I fear the day it happens
The day I fall apart
I've used up all my glue now
and painted out my heart.

–Margaret M. Cavaletto, © 1994

Looking back, I'm amazed at the concept of "pieces" portrayed in my poem since I had no understanding of dissociation or multiplicity. In that first visit to Mary, I learned more than I had learned in the previous eighteen months, or in twenty years of therapy. During those twenty years, I had covered the same problems, mostly dealing with depression and sexual dysfunction, over and over, with never any relief. Although I had been aware of a great deal of childhood physical, sexual, and psychological trauma, I had no inkling of its extent, or of my father's sexual abuse.

Mary explained that, although I had only fleeting memories of severe abuse, I most likely had a dissociative disorder. She explained to me the concept of the "revolving door syndrome," whereby various "personalities" or "ego states," thinking they are the only survivors, try to run the body, each one bumping into the other in their attempts to do so. To maintain sanity, depression will close the whole system down until something else can be done. She encouraged me to communicate with these "parts" by asking questions with my right (dominant) hand, and answering them with my left.

I was skeptical. I didn't believe I was "dissociative," "multiple," or any of the other things she mentioned. I was in such a state of liquefaction after my experiences with my husband, my earlier therapist, and all that I had endured, that it was more like the "blender blades," than revolving doors.

Then there were the drugs. My psychiatrist was a very easygoing fellow who had prescribed every combination of antidepressants he could think of, and then, for two years, every combination I suggested. His next step for me had been shock treatment, since I had failed to respond to any of the drugs. I refused shock treatment. When I began to see Mary, I was on maximum doses of both Prozac and Wellbutrin, all to no avail. Once I had an inkling of what my problem was, and how to go about "fixing it," I stopped seeing the psychiatrist. I had no insurance by then anyway. I decided to go against everyone's advice and stop taking the drugs.

I was highly suicidal. My only criteria was that it had to look like an accident for the sake of my sons. A friend had invited me to go to Mexico with her to visit her family for three weeks. I knew I couldn't kill myself while I was with her, so I left the remaining drugs at home and rode in the back seat of a pickup truck deep into Mexico. We lived in her home, one of the nicest in the pueblo. Although the floors were dirt and the running water was in the backyard, it had a bathroom. The one phone in town was very expensive. With no money, I had little to do with my days but to follow Mary's advice: write!

I was surprised at my writing. My left hand responded in the most unexpected ways, with the most amazing information. The "parts" identified themselves mostly as "ego states"; i.e. Faith, Fear, Love, Sad, Longing, Pretend, Fat, Humility, Lonely, Hope, Efficient (Fish), Depression (Deep). Then there were the individuals: Baby, protected by Sad; Little One, protected by Lonely; Boots (the angry one); and Julia, the evolved one, the Spiritual Goddess, the Wise One.

I will pick up my story, after my return from Mexico, with excerpts of letters written to my "pseudo parents" who live in St. George, Utah. I met them at church in San Francisco. Though I was married and twenty-six years old, they adopted me and have been loving supports ever since. Explaining things to them through my writing, was a wonderful exercise, because they knew little about my abuse.

MAY, 1995
Dear Ivan and Glenna:

It's amazing to me how much has happened, even since I wrote the letter I never mailed in February. One huge development is that my former therapist and psychiatrist both encouraged me to take a break from school because I was not capable of dealing with it. They were right. On the same Friday I decided to quit, an avalanche of new memories came. This set of memories boosted the severity of my abuse from "incest" to "sadistic abuse." My brother remembers things beyond my memories; he says the reason my dad sold me for so little per session is that he only wanted enough money to buy another fifth of whiskey.

Surprisingly, I find that comforting. At least it wasn't simply his disregard for my worth, but his poison that determined the asking price.

I have finally found a therapist who can explain to me the process I must go through and how to do so.

MEMORIAL DAY, 1995
Dear Ivan and Glenna,

Last Tuesday evening I came home from watching my kids at their dad's house. He has agreed to let me take care of them while he works. When I got home, I climbed into bed with the flu. I can remember being that sick only two or three times in my life. I likened myself to a weaving. I pictured my soul—the dynamic, eternally growing part of me, my intelligence—as an upward flowing tress of golden silky threads. They were smooth and vibrant. I pictured the side-to-side weaving materials as those placed by my parents initially, then others who came to influence the design and content of the fabric of my soul.

The feeling I had—sharp, painful, burning—was of having a fine-toothed comb placed at the roots of my soul, working out the snarls, carding out the lint and whatever else had been placed inappropriately there. I perceived that if I had been intended to be woven into silk or linen, my parents only had materials sufficient to weave me into a Kleenex!

This vision came as a result of trying to explain to an acquaintance why I was alone, without my boys, trying to piece myself back together. She was of the opinion that "it's all in the past, it's all over now, just get on with your life before you make that a permanent part of yourself. Rehashing it can only make it worse."

Of course she didn't grasp the concept, but it became more clear to me. My work is not only to allow myself to be cleansed of the lint and snarls of my past teachings, but to reweave the truth. If I were to simply comb over the top of all that, I would leave my intelligence there (at least the parts of me that were caught in the snarls and never allowed to grow).

Whereas most children automatically are taught that they are of some worth, of some value, of some joy, and can hope for better things for themselves, I was not. I was taught the opposite. Before I can progress in those areas, I must reweave the information I was given. Telling it to my present state-of-self doesn't count. The resulting decisions, subconscious decisions that inevitably result from such original information, can only be changed as the information is changed.

I just finished a particularly grueling memory that began with seven-year-old Little One having her legs tied to the legs of the kitchen table, bent over it, and sodomized by my father. He then turned me over and told me that since it was my shit that had gotten him dirty, I had to "clean him off" orally. My head was hanging backwards over the table, and he held a French knife to my throat, saying I was no bigger than a baby goat, and mom would think she was eating goat meat for dinner. The memory involved four of my alters in an ordeal that seemed to go on forever. When it was over, my father said he would kick the shit out of me if I told anyone. Why would I want to give him a reason to hate me more than he already did? I hated myself anyway.

The next few days were extremely difficult as I suffered "deep" depression, combined with seething anger. It had taken several days to get through the memories of this episode, and it took another several days to overcome their aftermath. During this period, I was introduced to a new part. I kept asking who had the memory and finally got the answer, "Wooden you like to know?" He (yes, I have several male parts), gave me some details and passed the baton to Deep.

As it turns out, Wooden was my catatonic state. As I was writing, I asked what happened next, and wrote "I became Wooden." Then I actually became catatonic—watched myself in the closet mirror as it happened. What an amazing thing the mind is. And going out of your mind isn't as difficult as you might think.

AUGUST 3, 1995
Dear Ivan and Glenna,

For many days, maybe weeks, I had been so depressed that I felt my prayers were lead balloons. Last week's depression was the aftermath of one, and precursor to another, set of unbelievable tortures. All I can say is, I'd rather be me than my dad and all his friends.

For a week, I processed memories of being eight years old (Little One), and spending a week with my dad. He worked during the day and left me tied on the bed, spread-eagle, while he was gone. While he was there, in the evening and through the night, he inserted popsicles, cucumbers, and himself in my lower orifices, leaving me sticky during the day. He said he was trying to stretch my entrances so I wouldn't cry when he and his friends entered. I couldn't swat at the ants and flies that crawled on my body.

As I write, I still have the sensation of the crawling bugs and an occasional insect bite. My insides are sore and my rectum is painful. These bodily sensations were saved until they could be manifested during this period of safety in my life. I'm grateful to be able to give them vent at last.

This was my first real experience with processing a memory almost completely in order to elicit the "BASK" model with awareness of *Behaviors*, emotional *Affect*, body *Sensations* and expression through abreaction, *Knowledge* and perception of my inner child's experience. It turned out not to be complete, as I needed "knowledge," and went into a dark, depressive state, staying in bed for two days.

I realized that part of the feelings of despair and loneliness belonged to the characters who were unable to express them years ago. I simply needed to hang with those feelings for a day or two. They had been sequestered for many years, and deserved a day to vent.

It seems so impossible that these things could have happened, but I cannot deny the testimony of my body and my detailed left-handed descriptions. I only write what comes. It flows—usually easily. When there is hesitation, it is frequently followed by more difficult information, which I would hesitate to describe, if I were telling the story.

The emotions I experience are also in synchronicity with the descriptions. How can I deny these calls for help from my long-tormented selves?

In group last week, I learned that depression is anger turned against the self. How can I rationally be angry with my magnificent self(ves)? With the help of God, who created my incredible mind, I have not only survived my dad's and his friends' brutal mistreatment, but I have excelled in many areas of accomplishment. As I continue to process the sewage my dad flushed into me, my waters will flow clear and pure and go forth to buoy and sustain others who need my help.

On the first Sunday in September, I finished my integration! I am no longer multiple! This is amazing and wonderful. It's been two weeks now and it's still holding. I'm one again!

In dialoguing with Lonely about her feelings, I became aware that although she had done much to protect us, she still felt so unloved and lonely that she wished she could die. I acknowledged her strength in being able to let me feel her so intensely, despite all the other feelings. "We must learn to let other feelings in. If we allow loneliness to be our focus, it will grow until that's all we are. I know you have other attributes—courage, compassion, protection, intelligence and humor." I suggested a renaming that would include all her traits. She became Laura.

Sad and Baby, who wanted to go to sleep and never wake up, were sometimes helped by angels. The angels would hold Baby when Sad hurt too much. Sad said that she always wanted to die because this place was hard, ugly, and sad.

My heart felt broken to hear how much Sad had suffered, how long she was neglected, and how I hadn't believed her, even hated her. I shared my appreciation and gratitude with them both, and wondered if the two of them would be willing to join as one now that their work of being a broken baby, and the protector of the baby was done. Sad and Baby became Sadie.

Laura had needed to be separate to protect Little One, and take over where Little One left off. By dividing, Laura helped make Little One stronger. Since the trauma was past, Laura and Little One could be more effective in synergy. They became Lauren.

We listed all the Fragments: Fat (Integrity), Broken, Pretend, Julia, Despair/Discouraged, Stupid, Hope/Faith, Fish. Anyone else?

Boots explained that he didn't keep all the awful experiences inside and he didn't tell about the really bad stuff, either. When I asked him if that didn't make him angry, he replied, "Yes, but that part wasn't safe to remember, let alone tell. And safe is more important than anger. I knew how to be safe, and still do."

Some were concerned that after holding the torturous pain, suffering, loneliness and despair all these years, that I would abandon them. I told them, "I will never abandon you again. No matter how involved we become in helping others I could never do without you. But I know we can't be successful until we are integrated, synergized, wholly one."

"What is stopping us from being one now," I wondered? "What more work do we need to do before we can become Margaret—my given name, the name I assumed we would be as a whole?"

Deep remained. He was no longer needed to protect us from the fear, anger, or overwhelming work. We needed his depth of character, faith, and desire to serve and protect, to stand for all we knew to be true. He expressed his willingness to do his part.

We were then ready to become one. I told them, "Not only have you preserved my eternal Self in the pristine condition in which it came from my Father, but you have each developed the strengths, talents, and abilities you uniquely offer to make me whole. We all know each step was guided and protected by our loving Heavenly Father, and that he has cultured me for his own purposes. We will need every ounce of that strength to accomplish the work He has for us. We are bound together as one again. I am Margaret, "the Pearl." The stones of adversity have been coated well, each layer adding to the strength and beauty of this precious Margaret!

I feel like a new person. My emotions are much more available to me. I miss my sons even more acutely. I am more functional than I have ever been, it seems. I spend long hours typing, trying to get this all recorded and out for the benefit of others.

SEPTEMBER 25, 1995
Dear Ivan and Glenna,

In the hospital (1992), a counselor put it to me this way:

"I have some good news and some bad news. The bad news is your parents didn't love you enough and never will. Nothing can or will ever change that. No amount of parenting given to you now will satisfy your abandoned inner child. Parental love can come only from outside your-self if the receiver is a child.

The good news is you can reparent that child, and there is nothing she can need or want that you can't give her."

Taking that one step further, I realized that all true parenting comes from Above; as children of God that involves learning the worth of a soul, learning first to love the self.

In the years that followed, I continued to heal, to grow, and to learn who I am and who I want to be. There came a day when I felt I had finished to the point where I could write the following epilogue to Porcelain Bisque:

Epilogue to Porcelain Bisque

Just as I had feared it would,
the day dawned bright and cold.
The glue could stick no longer
The seams all lost their hold.
At first I couldn't pick them up;
the pieces lay in shards, and
scattered to the blowing winds
like a deck of playing cards.

I searched at first halfheartedly,
not wanting to believe
the whispered scraps of evidence
my mind began to weave.

I only came to know the truth
by the Spirit's patient teaching,
by gentle words of kind reproach,
and time and time beseeching.

The Spirit taught me first to see
that to believe in God's great Gift,
I must, as well, give credence to
the great, eternal rift.

That I must first embrace the fact
that evil does bear sway,
in a world of relativity
where Love is the only way.

And then I tried to justify
the actions of my dad —
The teachings of his fathers
were what had made him bad.
The Voice then gently chided me,

and calling me by name,
He pointed out the obvious —
our teachings were the same.

And that became the turning point
from whence I understood —
it's not the circumstance that counts,
but the choice for ill or good.

At last I could believe the things
my pieces had to tell.
The psychic walls came tumbling down,
and the truth began to jell.

Those days were the loneliest
I hope I ever spend,
as I set forth to do the work
of helping myselves mend.

I gathered every single piece
and peeled the paint and glue;
uncovered all the hidden pain
and suffered it anew.

I took my pieces to the Lord
and laid them at his feet,
for I could find no mortal way
to make the edges meet.
I feared that I would ever be
in pieces on the floor
or that I'd have to wait till death
and rising, to be more.

But no. He gathered every piece
and held them to his breast,
infusing them with love and light,
till each formed with the rest.

He held me up to see myself
as I had been revamped.
In place of porcelain sugar bowl,
was a leaded crystal lamp.

My simple form was exquisite,
each facet catching light;
reflecting out to others who
were searching in the night.
A guiding light he made of me
and set me on a hill;
a sparkling beacon of His love,
for others broken still.

—Margaret M. Cavaletto, © *1996*

The story is far from over. In November of 1996, I discovered that my inner selves were able to retrieve more information by continuing in the left-hand writing mode when I wrote in my journal. I was so invested in being "INTEGRATED," that I was afraid to write with my left hand, yet "they" insisted on naming themselves, and became caustic about my denial of them. They finally used four colors of ink so they didn't have to be so formal about it. Each chose her/his own color so I could identify them as the original basic four: Julia, Lauren, Sadie, and Deep. Sometimes Fish spoke up, too.

I fought hard not to let them out. I was determined to be integrated; I wasn't about to acknowledge that I really was multiple. I don't quite understand why I was so invested in being integrated. In retrospect, I think I just wanted to be done, and to get on with life, as though what I was living was something else.

As I see it now, rather than being a detour in my life, every experience is a gift. Each opportunity to better know myself and create who I am, is more welcome now. I'm slowly learning, the hard way, that there's always more, and that I'll never be done, whole, or whatever, until I *am*. Or maybe I already *am*, and need to remember that more often.

In June of 1997, I traveled to Oregon for training in Rapid Eye Technology. Before I went, and when I first arrived, I noticed that unless I was with someone I really trusted, I did not respond to the sessions. I was discouraged, thinking that

Rapid Eye was ineffective. But when it was effective, it was awesome. On the first morning of the training, I was working with a fellow student and nothing was happening. I had been aware of Sadie's energy that whole weekend, so I told the student to ask for Sadie. She did, and I immediately responded. That was such a blow to me! I was in such denial about being truly multiple. I had been *integrated.* I knew that in my journal I still had parts, but I didn't take it literally. In response to this new Rapid Eye modality, though, I had a strong feeling that they were all lined up back there, saying, "Who, me?"

JOURNAL ENTRY: JUNE 18, 1997

I am learning more about how our system works (or doesn't work). I was excited to find that when we asked for Sadie, I was able to respond to the eye work.

Julia, who protected me as my Higher Self, came with Baby, the original self. Sad split off from Baby when Baby was nine months old. Mamma had left at that time and wouldn't nurse Baby any more. Julia watched over Baby and helped her from the outside.

"Who is Margaret?"

"Margaret is a name for the world to call us by."

There is a feeling of confusion and fear as I wonder who is asking the questions. Who doesn't believe all this? Is Julia the "Self," the one referred to in the book, Mosaic Mind, *by Richard Schwartz and Regina Goulding?*

Julia refused to respond because I was so distraught; she didn't want to make matters worse for me. I went to class that morning and felt scattered all over the room. I was in such a state of crisis—identity crisis.

In my next session with teachers at the Rapid Eye Institute, they called forth my parts, who expressed deep, sobbing grief. It came in nine waves, supposedly for nine different alters. Then they all circled in a dance, and took themselves to the light, leaving me aware only of Julia. I have a difficult time explaining the feeling that was left. Sometimes when I pray, or when I am especially close to Spirit, I have a feeling of being encased in a squooshy energy larger than myself that can be manipulated by me. I laid in this warm cocoon for a long time and didn't want to move.

In this state of bliss, I was aware of myself as Julia, and determined to change my name to Julia Fairchild. I didn't want my father's or my ex-husband's name, and chose instead to be a "fair daughter of God." I legally changed my name, but in retrospect, it seems that by having taken on the name of my higher self, I've put my Self in a bind. For one thing, it perpetuates my problem of not being grounded, bypassing my "emotional self," or "ego," and assuming I'm something higher. It seems to defeat my purpose of having a mortal experience. It is also confusing. I communicate with my higher Self as "me," but use the name, Julia. "I" am the liquid crystal whole. I am Margaret and Julia, the soul, the spirit, the mind and the body (heart, liver, spleen, lungs, etc.). I've finally decided to take the name "Margaret" as my given name because it represents "Margaret is," without having to use the name under which I suffered so much. It is unfortunate that, for the purposes of writing a book, one must attempt to freeze in words, events that continue to be dynamic.

One month later, I finally got the courage to ask, left-handed, if I was truly integrated. The answer was: "As integrated as anyone ever is. Those who served you in trauma are truly synergized into the wholeness of Margaret, the original daughter, the grown woman."

The difference in me was tangible, and many of my friends and loved ones noticed that I was more mature, more calm and at peace.

It seems to me that integration comes in three stages and that Dissociative Identity Disorder perfectly describes those stages. Stage One, healing the dissociation, involves recovery and processing of the lost memories—fitting the puzzle back together. I have been asked for my definition of the difference between synergy and integration. To me, integration is accomplished in the first stage of healing: information gathering, BASK modeling, integration of previously scattered material. It is the process of putting together the circumstances, retrieving the memories and integrating them into the wholeness of experience that caused the splits in the first place. Integration also involves discovering the parts, and identifying their roles, and even the preliminary introduction of the parts to each other and to the whole of the system.

Synergy, on the other hand, is the process of blending similar parts, combining efforts of cooperation and eventual joining to become the whole. As the term suggests, it is the process by which the sum of the parts becomes capable of achievements of which each is individually incapable. It could be related to Stage Two, which involves overcoming the identity crisis: deciding who is who, and who does what, and establishing communication and cooperation between the parts. It may or may not involve total integration. It may involve melding of certain parts, like Little One and Lonely, or Baby and Sad. A final phase of that stage may involve total integration, which seems to be different for everyone. I still feel myself to be Me, Myself, and I. Me represents left-brain, cognitive thinking; Myself is right-brain, subconscious, imagination, feeling mind (Margaret); and I Am, is that part of the whole, the collective unconscious as expressed in me as the spirit, Julia, which I see to be where the seams meet on the blanket of humankind.

Stage Three I see as the process of bringing order to disorder—of creating day-to-day life from the new perspective and experiences of the synergized person (however that may show up). I don't believe it was ever intended for there to be just One, at least as a mortal experience. We are equipped with a higher self, and an ego or emotional, experiential (mortal) self. Of course, mortality is an illusion, a temporary experience of an immortal being. But duality, relativity, separation of those selves is important for the purposes of mortal experience.

It has been said that a "normal" person begins therapy at the point of integration. Having fit the pieces back together again does not mean that those experiences have been less damaging to the development, or that missing developmental stages have been remedied. I'm sure there is much left to do in coming to terms with the reality of a lost childhood.

I am now in the third stage of the healing process: bringing order to my life and, what's more, filling the void that was the trauma. I still journal with both hands. Julia, the mind, writes with the right hand. Julia, heart and soul, writes with the left. I still don't have cognition of heart and soul without writing, but I wonder if anyone does? I think rather than being "split," I simply have found doors to my inner selves that others may not be aware they have. Julia, the heart, put it this way in my journal:

The others are here, part of the whole, but no more separate parts. We have all of their everything, but the pain and trauma has changed and gone to the light. What is missing is positive experience to take its place. So, in some respects, I feel empty, devoid of experience. Without the others, I also sometimes feel sad and lonely, and somewhat hollow and fragile.

Julia the soul writes:
You need to feed me. I am starving.
What do you eat?

Rainbows, music, sunsets, fresh air, good books, prayer, walks in the early morning, friends who love me, reading to the children, solitude, peaceful moments, unconditional love, candlelit baths, green things, dancing, drumming, helping others, writing, singing, gardening, ceramics, art, cleanliness and order. When these basic foods are plentiful, I will be more help to you. I am weak now.

What is it that I feel? I am crying without words. I have a deep sense of something I can't identify without writing about it. When I ask, I understand that the crying is about hope, longing, sorrow that we are yet so fragile and weak, and joy that we are finding each other and communing. Keep writing. Keep listening. Keep loving.

How do I function differently? I feel voracious for input. I've done a few things I never would have done before for the sake of experience. I feel a little like Johnny 5 in the movie, *Short Circuit.* "Input, input, input!"

I've changed churches, which surprises me. I was such a good little Mormon. The straight lines and boundaries the church set for me, however, saved my life. Because I was so straight, I didn't get involved in drugs or promiscuity. The paradigm of Mormonism fit while I was healing, but I am more confused now as to who or what God really is. All I know is that God Is. While the spirituality of it is real for me, I never fit as a molly Mormon—more like a Zen Mormon. So now I'm going to a more metaphysical mode.

One other change is that when I was healing, I was rabid to become a healer. While I haven't changed my mind, I'm not so driven anymore. I feel more confident that each person can find his or her own way, that I am only one leaf upon the tree, and that God has it all in hand. I can offer the shade of which I am capable, but God plants and waters the trees. I've also learned that all you get for chasing ambulances is tired. Each individual comes to her own healing in her own time. I can stay on my own path and trust that if anyone crosses it, it was meant to be.

The narrative could have ended there, but two significant incidents have since occurred which shed more light on the ongoing process of integration. After my experience in Oregon, which was highly significant, a friend who practices kinesiology and hypnosis, came to give a weekend workshop, and stayed in my home. I had several sessions with him, and at the end of the weekend, he tested my muscles with the question of whether or not I had been abused by my father. The answer was NO!

I had never felt so betrayed, confused, humiliated, and heart-broken as at that moment. I was able, after a great deal of soul searching, to come to some peace, at least cognitively. I was certain that whether or not it happened, I knew and loved my parts. I got what I needed from their experiences, but had to conclude that perhaps they had made up the circumstances to teach me what I needed to know. It is said that the body never lies, so my question was, "Which time did it lie? The times I was abreacting such graphic portrayal of my abuse, or the time I tested negative about my father's abuse having happened?" One curious thing was that when my body was asked if I had been abused by my dad, the answer was no; when my body was asked if my writings were true, the answer was yes. Needless to say, I was highly confused, and extremely depressed. Because the veracity of my experience was in question, I lost faith in my ability to write, pray or receive any true answers. I felt as if I was in a freefall into a black hole.

A month passed, and I went to the conference in San Francisco on "Wholeness and Multiplicity," where I was so richly fed. While I was there, I was even more confused and filled with grief. I had a sense of belonging and fitting in on the one hand, and a sense of betrayal and rejection on the other. The answer finally came as I stood alone in the parking lot after the conference. A tiny wisp of voice came to my mind, and said, "Julia wasn't there." Even now as I write, the relief of that moment floods over me again. What a gift!

What this has come to mean to me, on the other side of the hill, is that I am no longer trauma-based. The others took the trauma to the light. If I had been skeptical of the efficacy of Rapid Eye before, I'm a believer now. Julia wasn't one of those who was directly traumatized. When they were all taken "to the light," Julia was left. But those who had been traumatized were no longer operating at the trauma-based cellular level. That was explained earlier, where the alters came in nine waves, grieved, and then circled and danced to the light in a Rapid Eye session. It is said that Rapid Eye Technology actually changes emotions at a cellular level, and that new neural pathways are developed, exactly as in REM sleep. This seems to have been the case with my experiences.

Just like the experience of being told that none of it ever happened, and believing it, and then the joyful relief of finding out the truth, I would never have known the truth if it hadn't been brought into question, and if I hadn't suffered so. It means so much more to me now, knowing that Julia wasn't there. The significance of that is monumental, but wouldn't have been if I had not had that painful experience. I rejoice in every experience. If there were no darkness, there would be no need for light.

I magine my surprise, then, to have been faced with the next significant incident. A close friend/therapist told me that it was time I stopped isolating and started dating. So, after a hectic quarter of school, I answered a classified ad and made arrangements for my first date since the divorce three years earlier. I talked to the man on the phone for three hours on Friday night. He knew all the right things to say, all the detours to my heart, all the lonely places to fill. I felt so excited and hopeful to finally be heard and understood by a man. I looked forward with joyful anticipation to the following day when we had a date.

The reality was quite another story. We met at my office on a Saturday, then went to the group room. Although there were usually people there, no one was around that day. The man had only one agenda, and that was to have sex—immediately. I had made it perfectly clear to him that I wasn't interested in sex until I was familiar with, and comfortable in, the relationship. The minute I saw him, my flags went up; he had a huge beard and, to me, facial hair is reminiscent of pubic hair. I told him that his beard was offensive to me, as was the fact that he smoked a pipe and his teeth were grungy. I said I wasn't interested in having sex with him, or probably even going out with him again.

Ignoring all I said, he bent me over backwards on a couch and began to kiss me. The minute his beard was in my face, I became Little One. I immediately reverted to all my old coping mechanisms. I did what I was told. I expected to take it to the inevitable conclusion, and I wanted to get it over with.

Of special interest to me was the fact that every aspect of the childhood incident on the kitchen table was present in this set of circumstances. When I was abused as a child, there was anal and oral penetration. The man's beard seemed exactly like the pubic hair my dad tortured me with. The man was impotent, so it took two-and-half-hours (forever) for me to get him hard enough to ejaculate, which he forced me to do orally. It was like being back on that childhood table in nearly every way.

I think more devastating than being raped, was realizing how vulnerable I was to splitting again. I had no idea how quickly and easily that could happen. I had no idea that I was "an accident waiting to happen," and that I simply wasn't safe as long as that was the case. Of course, during the assault, I didn't know I was acting like seven-year-old Little One. It was only afterwards, when I sought professional help, that my friends recognized that I had split. Deep returned to manage for a few days. During the police examination, the officer, who had never dealt with multiplicity, quickly recognized when to hand me the teddy bear, and when to assure me in other ways. She was surprised and worried when I became catatonic for twenty minutes.

The man was a previously convicted sexual predator, and knew exactly what he was looking for in me. Hindsight tells me that he intended to do exactly what he did from the time he placed the ad, and that I fit all his criteria. Being overweight, he assumed my self-esteem was so low that I wouldn't follow through in the prosecution. That may have been true of Little One, but Margaret is another story. I (Margaret) dialogued with Deep, Julia, and Little One to come to agreement about what to do regarding prosecution. Of course, we all decided to press charges and prosecute. It later became apparent that Lauren had split again, and that Lonely and Little One were no longer integrated. It seems that Lonely felt responsible for getting us into that position in the first place, and that Little One felt responsible for handling the sexual duties of the system. She felt that Margaret, who wasn't there, wouldn't know how to handle sex. Lonely went into hiding and didn't surface for several weeks. Little one was very apparent in those weeks, and Deep came out whenever he was needed for strength, or in stressful situations.

Since the spring of '98, I have found myself to be more fragile. When I am especially tired or stressed, my parts become discernible to those who know me well.

I don't know what this means in the larger picture of integration after multiplicity. I believe it happens differently for every person, and that my experience could possibly help someone to be more aware and self protective. After the initial devastation and splitting, which was quite severe and lasted about two weeks, I quickly bounced back to normal life and felt that I had gained more than I had lost in the experience. Without it, I might have taken longer to face the issues surrounding my sexuality, vulnerability, and integrity.

With regard to integrity, it occurred to me that a similar incident had occurred months before, but the man had been so gentle, I hadn't even realized that it was a rape. This experience helped me to see that, in regard to my sexuality, the weaving of the basket I call "integrity" has a huge hole in it. A gentle rape was like having a softball thrown through the hole. It took a basketball-sized experience—a brutal rape—to let me know how lacking I am in the integrity that I would like to have surround my sexuality. After all, when would I have had the opportunity to weave a tight understanding of what sexuality means to me, or where my boundaries are, or to learn how to conduct myself in any way resembling an adult woman?

I have much to learn from this experience, as I do from all the others I've encountered. I'm grateful for the opportunity for growth.

I've been asked to define forgiveness. When I place myself in the larger picture, understanding that it's not what happens to you but how you allow it to affect you, harboring bitterness or unforgiving makes no sense. The only feeling I can muster for perpetrators is compassion, sorrow, pity. To be so desperate that they have to grab whatever it is they're after in their over-indulgence and cruelty, must be a terrible way to live.

In the larger picture, knowing as I do that there has to be someone to hold the darkness so the light can shine against it, I honor the sacrifice it must have taken for these people to sink so deeply into darkness as to completely lose sight of the light. I'm grateful they were willing to give that much so that I could measure myself against their darkness. I'd much rather be the victim than the perpetrator; and, in the largest scheme of things as I see them, there is no such thing as either.

I can honestly say that, for me, there is nothing to forgive. I would not change one day of my life. I have come to love myself more, and to value the parts of me that endured unspeakable circumstances with nobility, courage, innocence, and valor. Although I wouldn't wish my experiences on my friends or my children, without them I would never have known and loved myself the way I do. My experiences brought out the best in me.

Elizabeth

Throughout most of my deepest recovery, I worked full time, except for nine months when I was between jobs. I now work as a sales representative for an HMO, an industry that is undergoing the stress of many changes. Since my integration, I contribute more fully at my job, and am better able to cope with my life. On my most recent evaluation, I received an outstanding rating for interpersonal relations. However, the most important thing of all is that I have a satisfying relationship with myself.

Most of my life I believed I came from a fairly normal family. My mother was a teacher. My father was first a farmer and later a factory worker. Like many other farmers and factory workers, he frequented the taverns after work and spent hours drinking with his friends on weekends. When I recognized that I, too, had a problem with alcohol and sought help for it, I began to think that Dad was not just a garden variety alcoholic.

My sister Jane, who is retarded, developed severe emotional problems. As she grew older, she became more and more emotionally labile and demanding. If not given what she wanted, when she wanted it, she would go into a rage no matter where she was. She was totally unable to control herself in public. She was not able to devise a way to cope with life's demands and so has never had a life of any quality. She is now completely physically disabled.

My first glimpse of what a loving family might be like was

portrayed on Ozzie and Harriet with the Nelson family. I was twelve when I saw that show for the first time. I watched it open-mouthed because the father actually talked to his sons. I didn't know fathers would do that. My own father rarely talked to me except to criticize or scold, and he never touched me except to abuse me.

Nearly six years after my father died, I entered therapy at the age of forty-eight.

JOURNAL ENTRY: SPRING 1989
Dear Inner Self:

I feel as if I am on the brink of major discoveries about myself. As if something is going to open up, some way to find an explanation, some way to make sense of things … I want to get to the bottom of this, to put all the red flags together and wave them.

About six months later, the memories started to surface, one by one, somewhat fuzzy at first. I learned that when I wanted to bring a memory into focus, I could allow myself a quiet time to go into a trancelike state and journey inward. I would write in my journal and the details would appear on the paper.

JOURNAL ENTRY: AUGUST 29, 1989
Dear Inner Self:

I feel as though the onion is peeling, as though I am living my life backwards. I am about two years old and the memory of sitting on Dad's lap is fuzzy. He is trying to console me. There is blood on his hands. I am inconsolable, but I am feeling he is all I have—that I have to accept his attention, for there is nothing else. My mother isn't there. I can't tell anyone what is happening. I am feeling responsible, as though I am attracting sexual abuse, like flies to fly paper. I feel defective, dirty … I feel responsible, taking on responsibility for an emotionally ill, disturbed adult. I am two years old, a little innocent child, a baby.

I have come to realize that the abuse in my family was extreme. As I pieced my memories together, I got the strong feeling that I might have come from a transgenerational Satanic Cult family. From a variety of sources, I came to recognize signs, first of ritual abuse and later of Satanism in my family. Many of my memories took place in a barn on our farm in the Midwest, a remote rural setting. My father was always the leader. In my earliest memories of rituals in the barn, there were crowds of faceless people standing around a crude altar, upon which the victim lay. At first, I saw only the faces of my immediate family. As I progressed in recovery, I saw the faces of aunts and uncles on both sides of the family. There were many secrets: abuse directed towards me; crimes against others, like sacrifices of infants and murders of children and adults. I do not believe that anyone was ever arrested. As a child, I could do nothing except take care of myself by splitting.

During the rituals, murders were committed, as well as heinous forms of abuse and human sacrifices. The one that gave me the greatest grief was remembering my father choking an old man to death. The old man's eyes fixed on me pleadingly. I suffered agonizing guilt for not having been able to help him.

As I heard and read about Satanism, I learned that certain holidays are common to Satanic cults. I was startled to notice that my birthday, and those of my brother and sisters, fell on those days. I was born on September 22, my brother on March 21 (spring equinox), my younger sister on September 21 (fall equinox), and my older sister on April 25 during "preparation for sacrifice," (from April 21–26, a time of preparing for holidays which take place from April 26–May 1). Additionally, my brother's daughter and my sister's ex-husband have birthdays on September 22. My sister married on September 22, as well. So many coincidences! I have pondered this and wondered if there was some planning involved to make it all happen on those dates. I have no answers except the knowledge that, as I mentioned above, these are often important days to those who practice Satanism.

The rituals were highly planned and held in the evening, with an attendance of about a dozen people. These took place Saturday nights, mainly in spring or fall. My parents were as scrupulous about the Satanic rituals as they were about their Catholic rituals. At the Satanic rituals, there was always some form of altar, table, or something improvised such as sawhorses supporting wooden planks. My father was always the leader, with everyone else standing around in a circle. I suspect there was also some use of drugs because everyone seemed to be in a trancelike state, with their faces expressionless. In their Catholic religiosity, my parents followed all the Catholic rules: no meat on Fridays, mass attendance every Sunday and all Christian holy days. There was no reconciliation of the conflicting doctrines. It was as though we were two different families, the Satanic family, and the Catholic family.

An early memory of the abuse was of seeing myself being ritually tortured by my father when I was about eighteen months old. I was tied "spread eagle" on a bed and he was inserting an object in and out of my vagina. I can still see my little baby-like legs. My father had a completely blank expression on his face. My face was also blank and very pale. I was watching this from the ceiling. I had "split" and left my body, enabling me to be in two places at once. Incredible! This was my first cognitive memory of an abuse ritual so painful, so awful, that the only way I could tolerate it was for another personality, an alter, to form. I became Cindy. When I became another personality, I not only felt numb but was suddenly relieved of tremendous pain. I was removed from myself, as though watching someone else's life. I became aware that my alters would come out, one at a time, and take over my body.

Later, I recovered a memory of near suffocation by both of my parents using a pillow. I was about three months old. Baby Susan came out to take over for the terrified little baby who was ready to give up and die. I believe part of the family's ritual abuse plan was to teach me how to dissociate, or split. A child who does not learn to split cannot be trusted to keep the family secrets. Even at the tender age of three months, I was bright and creative enough to instinctively find a way to cope.

Over the years of recovering memories by going into a trance, with and without the help of my therapist, and through writing, so many horrendous incidents came to consciousness that I was able to account for the development of thirteen different personalities and able to name each one. At the age of eight months, my mother battered me. She became frustrated with my crying. I was in my crib, rocking back and forth on "all fours," crying in sympathy for my brother, who was about seven years old. Mother was doing something to him and he was screaming in pain. Suddenly, she swung at me repeatedly with something in her hand like a mallet. She battered my right side until she fractured my right arm and possibly my jaw. When the pain became too intense to bear, Jennifer appeared for the first time and took over.

Many times during my recovery process I doubted myself. I thought, "I must be making all of this up, it couldn't be. No family could have lived such a secret life." My mother was a respected Catholic School teacher. We did things that other families did. Look at the family pictures. See, we were a normal family. I finally looked at the family pictures closely and saw them for the first time. I saw the distancing, the depression, and the body language. I saw the stiff postures and the eyes turned sideways. I saw that we were not a normal family. I had been deceiving myself.

A friend in a 12-Step program told me that there would come a time when there would be irrefutable evidence of the abuse and that I would have to believe myself. That time came in July 1992. On an X-ray taken when I had fractured my right shoulder, there was a marking on my upper right arm—a scar left by an old fracture. This validated my memory of the fractured right arm from my mother beating me when I was eight months old. I believed myself.

About a year later, when I was looking through my old photo album, I saw my first communion picture the way it actually was: a thin, small girl wearing a white dress—not a very pretty dress. It wasn't satin and full like the other little girls' dresses. It was too sheer and too long. The length covered some of the multiple bruises on the spindly legs. Suddenly I saw more irrefutable evidence. I noticed for the first time that in the picture my right thumb nail was black. Then I remembered that I had had a black thumb nail for a long time. Shortly before that, I had recovered a memory of my father driving a nail through my right thumb because I wasn't cooperating with an abuse ritual. During that ritual, Sarah, age seven, came out and took over. My father frequently commented that "Elizabeth has spunk." He was seeing Sarah who did indeed have spunk. His abuse was so extreme she had to have spunk; it was a matter of life or death.

In the fall of 1992, I was laid off my job and unemployed for eight months. During those eight months, my personal growth accelerated. Just before that Christmas, I had a dream about having ear surgery without anesthesia. The dream turned out to be a predictor of what was to come. I began to hear the voices of my personalities, one by one. I heard them loud and clear. There was nothing to anesthetize me, neither alcohol nor any more denial. My therapist supported me while I related what was happening. I knew from others in my 12-Step group that many of these voices were multiple personalities. I had thought that somehow I had escaped that kind of reaction to the abuse. I had been in denial that I was different!

In December 1992, I wrote in my journal about "opening Pandora's box," saying that if I didn't open the box, I would never find the hope that was deep within it. I was beginning to understand the true richness of recovery, the need to go deeply into myself and find out who I truly was. Recovery for me is about changing all of my old ideas about myself and everyone around me.

In January 1993, I received a gift of obsidian from a relative in Mexico. Obsidian is associated with spiritual healing. In my journal I wrote, "It seems to be symbolic of a new phase of healing, real healing with hope." That heralded the beginning of a new period for me, one where I became acquainted with all thirteen of my personalities. I began by writing to the ones I knew about first. They wrote back with their left hands. I wrote to the youngest ones, but they were too young to write to me. As each personality surfaced, I worked on memories associated with them. I allowed myself to remember the incidents of abuse, then the feelings. The facts usually preceded the feelings. I went through days of feeling grief and great bursts of anger. I met with my therapist on Saturdays when we could have the building to ourselves, so I could pound and shout until I was nearly exhausted. At home, too, I pounded a pillow with a plastic bat, over and over. With the coming to consciousness of all the memories and the feelings that I had held down for so many years, I felt as if I was shoveling garbage out of a bottomless pit. For months it seemed as though garbage was my only legacy from my family.

When I broke my denial about the multiplicity, I began to notice strange things, such as having losses of a few minutes here and there. I once left a parking lot in San Francisco with keys still in the open trunk door of my car. I found out what I had done when I returned and the parking lot attendant said, "Hey lady, do you know how you left your car?" That shocked and puzzled me. How could I leave my car like that? I realized that I did not remember the time span from starting to open the trunk until I was in the building and in the elevator. Brief instances of lost time sometimes were triggered by a car trunk or a case, such as a briefcase. I learned not to panic, but to stop and ask myself what the trigger incident was.

In this particular instance, I remembered that when I was thirteen, I saw my father and other men remove an unconscious teenage girl from our car trunk. She was later murdered in the basement of our house and an article of her clothing was kept in a duffel bag in our attic. I have documentation of her disappearance and suspected murder from a number of newspapers. Once I recovered that memory, I was able to understand why I "split" when I took my brief case out of the trunk. I stopped keeping the case in the trunk. Sheila was the personality who formed to cope with the trauma of seeing that murder. Later, I wrote to Sheila.

Dear Sheila:

You aren't inferior to anyone. If you had had a better family you would have felt much better about yourself. There wasn't, and still isn't, anything wrong with you. You are a bright, attractive, talented fourteen-year-old girl, who deserves fulfillment and happiness. I will make sure that you get it.

Love, Elizabeth.

Because my father and brother were among my abusers, Mike was created to provide a supportive, loving male for me when I was entering adolescence. He was there to approve of me and to be the brother my own brother could never be. I trusted Mike and knew that I could count on him. The beauty of creating Mike was that I could then meet my own needs for approval, at least to some extent. However, nothing can take the place of a loving nuclear family.

I now know that my resourcefulness enabled me to create alter personalities who took over whenever the abuse became so severe that I could tolerate it no longer. Each personality developed her or his own thoughts, feelings and desires. This scenario took place thirteen times. My state of multiplicity is further evidence to me of the abuse. It has helped me believe the abuse really happened.

I learned from my therapist about working out agreements with my various personalities. I would promise my personalities that I would meet their needs in the evenings and on weekends in exchange for being able to go to work without them coming out at odd or inappropriate times. I would write them individually to ask what I could do for them, then plan a time to do it. Sometimes I would ask one of the older ones to care for the younger ones. For example, I asked Mike to spend time with Sarah and Laura, six and eight, because they adored Mike.

Louise's twelve-year-old ways of handling situations did not work in a business setting. She was formed to help cope with moving from one state to another, from an isolated farm to a small town, and with the disappointment I felt when I realized that the abusive behavior did not stop with our move. Louise, being very outspoken, served me well in a new school, but not as an adult. As I often switched personalities at times of great stress, Louise would sometimes come out unexpectedly and make inappropriate comments during discussions, or when I was in front of a group giving a presentation. I would feel a little shaky, similar to when I feel mildly hypoglycemic and need to eat. Then there would be a shift and I would feel different, usually more serious and somewhat ill at ease. I had to learn to meet her needs, and the needs of the other personalities, before the tension built up and someone would burst out at an inappropriate time.

There were happy moments, too, as I worked to meet the needs of each of my personalities. They all had names, but I don't know where the names came from. I addressed each one by whatever name came to me. I took them, usually one at a time, for outings. I went to Macy's and felt the soft baby clothes in lovely pastel colors for the infants. I spent hours looking for pretty dresses for each of the children. I picked out interesting things for the adolescents. I borrowed my son's sports car so that Mike could take it out for a drive. I went to the park and rode the merry-go-round with an adult friend who did not care why I wanted to go; she just loved merry-go-rounds. I visited the zoo with the same friend. I read *Little House on the Prairie* for Laura and Sarah who loved it. I bought a Cinderella coloring book and colored for Beth, who loved Cinderella and her beautiful gowns. I also bought cologne and lip gloss that a twelve-year-old would like, and wore it at home in the evenings.

I spent time almost every evening meeting the needs of one or more personalities. This required many hours of solitude. I was grateful that my outer children were grown and away from home and that my husband had a very busy schedule and did not notice some of my interests, such as coloring in a Cinderella coloring book!

I always knew when I was not giving someone enough time.

I would develop an inner tension, a signal of slight pain similar to what I imagine an electrical current would feel like. I felt different personalities in different places in my head. For example, I associated Susan with the back, right, top area of my head. When she needed my attention, that was where I felt the pain—nowhere else.

I have come to realize that all of my personalities had special talents and that those talents are still with me. Marcy loved to dance. It was her ability that made it enjoyable to learn ballroom dancing. Mike's mechanical ability made it possible for me to learn to operate a computer, a VCR and a camcorder. I believe that I am more versatile than most people because of the multiplicity. As a supervisor once said to me, "You do so many things so well." Another supervisor told me that she would like to "clone" me. That would have been some clone!

The beginning of my integration process was the middle of a long road to completeness. All my life I had felt not just inadequate but incomplete, like something vital was missing. I wanted to integrate and recapture the wholeness that had been destroyed shortly after my birth. My family had spent years taking me apart. I was like a puzzle that had been thrown to the winds. My personalities were one-dimensional people trying to function as complete human beings, but none could do it alone. It was time to retrieve the pieces of that large, complex puzzle and put them back together into one personality, reuniting all of the separate personalities with a central or core self who was still intact despite all I had been through.

From a book I read about multiplicity, I learned that one path to integration is for all the different personalities to experience chronological growth—to "age up." They needed to pass through the years along the way to adulthood. Each was the age I was at the time of the trauma that precipitated their development. As I met their needs, I would suddenly realize that they were developing and maturing. I made choices for them. I gave them the best of everything. In my mind's eye, I gave them loving parents and grandparents, choosing people whom

I knew and respected to fill those roles. I had a book of house designs and I chose various homes where they lived with their parents.

JOURNAL ENTRY: JANUARY 19, 1994
Dear Inner Selves (Mike, Marcy, Pat, Sheila, Megan, Louise, Ellen, Laura, Sarah, Beth, Cindy, Jennifer, and Susan):

Everything, and everyone, inside seems quieter. I believe that what is happening is that we are all coming closer together. At times I feel tension but not conflict. There is a peaceful kind of sadness. The sadness, I believe, is the loss of independence and strong individuality that I have enjoyed in all of you, almost as if you really were separate persons, but I know that you are separate personalities all in one body.

The process of "aging up" took all of them to college age. They went off to whatever college they wanted. That was their parting as independent personalities. I had granted each of them the opportunity to return as a separate personality—separate from the others and from my core personality, Elizabeth. I wanted to be certain that I did not try to rush integration.

As each one left for college, I felt grief. I then realized that this was a happy occasion, a sign that I had been successful in meeting their needs so they could grow up. All of my personalities are still available. My experience is that they are all behind me, standing and watching in a group, contented and together. I visualize them as though they are in a family portrait, although they have not come out since my integration.

Susan was the one who needed the most attention and took the longest to integrate. She was the artistic part of me I did not know I had. She enjoyed my oldest daughter, who also is artistic, admiring her style and wanting to be like her. She stayed alone, as a separate personality, for a prolonged period of time, including Christmas of 1996 in order to be with my daughter. She also stayed around until I got the dining room and living room furniture updated. Susan said my seventy's furniture was a disgrace! She also didn't like my conventional style of dress.

Because of Susan, I am becoming more relaxed about how I dress and am seeking a style that is more my own, rather than dressing in the safest fashion.

My final integration was gradual, with less and less contact with Susan—who was the last to integrate—until, finally, I felt whole and complete. Since that Christmas of 1996, Susan has not appeared as an individual, nor has anyone else. I became fully integrated in 1997, and the integration has held.

In 1989 when I started my deepest recovery, I remembered things and events I had suppressed for decades. Many things about myself started to make sense. I grew to understand why I hated and feared my father so much. I had suffered tremendous guilt for these feelings. I thought I was disobeying the fourth commandment: "Honor thy father and thy mother." At the same time, I never had any illusions about my relationship with him. Once in a while, I felt love for him, the desperate love of a child who craves nurturing. When my father died, I felt relieved. I realized that he could never again hurt me.

I felt very little for my mother when she died, although I missed her companionship. We had done mother-daughter things together, like shopping and sitting around the kitchen table talking and having coffee together. I did not experience real grief for either of them at their deaths. I did, however, experience grief for the parenting I did not receive. As each died, the hope of receiving parenting from either of them also died.

I believe they have tried to reach me from their after-death world and that they both want my forgiveness. At times I feel some degree of forgiveness; however, I am not ready to fully forgive either one of them. Forgiveness, for me, is letting go of the anger, pain and bitterness from the past. When I am able to do that, it will be to further my healing, for my own inner peace.

Because I was forced to split at such an early age, I had no recollection of what it was like to be whole. Being an integrated personality is a new experience for me. I have more energy. In the past, I required eight or nine hours sleep, but now I need less. It is easier for me to stay focused. I no longer start multiple projects and then struggle to complete them all. I am more confident. I am more secure in speaking my opinions. I no longer quietly go my own way when I do not agree. I am less embarrassed when I make a mistake.

I am less fearful in every area of my life. Several years ago, I took an intensive self-defense class where I had the opportunity to act out a personal scenario in which I stood up to my father and did not allow him to abuse me. I have been able to transfer to many life situations the healing that scenario provided. I am much safer in my body out in public and I am confident that I can defend myself from an attacker in most situations.

Most of all, I have confidence in my own intuition. Time and again, I make decisions based on what feels right. I gather information and instinctively decide what to do.

During the years previous to recovery, I was in a survival struggle. Even though I had moved two thousand miles away from my family and had little to do with them, the wounds still crippled me. I tried so hard to do everything right, to look good, be a perfect wife and mother, and to live up to everything expected of me by the Catholic Church. I learned that not only was that futile, it was not humanly possible. I knew absolutely nothing about the support that I needed and deserved. My poor fragmented self tried to do everything.

Healing has made it possible for me to move further out into the world. I have become more aware of everything around me. My relationships with family and friends are vastly improved, and I have a better understanding of healthy and unhealthy sexuality. Most of all, I can count on myself. Everything is clearer. Decisions come easier. I trust myself more than I do other people; I trust myself to know my own mind. My short term memory has improved. This amuses me because it is occurring in middle age when most people's short term memory is getting shorter! My children have let me know that they can count on me now. In turn, I do not have to try to control them because I feel so out of control. It is easier for me to accept them the way they are.

My relationship with my husband is much better. He is on

his own path to recovery. I see in him fragmentation that was once similar to my own. He has much difficulty remembering where he places things and cannot remember names of people he has met repeatedly. Conversations with him require me to explain things that he ought to remember.

From experience, I learned that it was best not to share very much with him. After having told him about my father raping me, he got angry and shouted, "You fucked your father." The first time he said that, I felt crushed and humiliated. I thought I had given him ammunition to abuse me again. In a way, I had. I had to learn to look elsewhere for support. He was not a safe person. The second time, I shouted back, "No, he fucked me and you had better get that straight! There is a big difference." With the guidance of my support system, I was setting limits and getting out of the role of victim. We do not have conversations like this anymore. I will not allow it. I am a worthwhile person who expects to be respected.

During my years of employment, I have worked under several highly dysfunctional managers. Each time I found myself under another "crazy boss," I would hope that somehow things would change. I have learned that there are many crazy bosses out there and I must learn to take care of myself. I must teach them to treat me with respect. I am able now to confront situations and take risks, as I can set limits and tell people what those limits are. If a situation cannot be improved, I remind myself that it is only a job and concentrate more on outside interests.

As part of learning what it is like to be an integrated personality, I discovered that there are different aspects of a normal personality. These aspects of me are not separate parts developed in response to abuse, but, rather, tapes developed from the voices of authority figures in my growing years. As I have gotten to know my new self, I have identified parts of me that I call "the pusher," "the critic," and several others. In order to get acquainted, I have worked on making friends with these parts. I am working to turn the critic into a supporter. The critic is like my older sister. She wants me to succeed and so she watches my every move to the point where she paralyzes me with criticism. With much effort, the critic is becoming my champion when I do things well, which also allows me to make mistakes.

I have also healed physically. I had developed a chronic infection in my right thumb, the same thumb my father had driven a nail through so long ago. Although my thumb has completely healed after multiple surgeries, I believe the infection was from a body memory of the original abuse. This was also true of a fractured right shoulder I sustained in a fall early in recovering my memories. I have many memories of abuse of my right arm and shoulder: a beating by my mother when I was eight months old; my father sometimes dragging me by my right arm. Occasionally, I still get a faint body memory, although I have not had a new cognitive memory in a year or more.

January 1998 marked almost nine years since the beginning of my deep recovery. At that time, I realized I had become comfortable being myself–the person I had always wanted to be. The process of recovering my memories and learning about my multiplicity has allowed me to appreciate my intelligence, my creativity, and myself. It has given me confidence beyond that of being a survivor of horrendous abuse.

The integration itself was a long three-year process. I am glad I made the decision to integrate, and am grateful for my loving support system and the resources I have found. To anyone who is wondering if it is all worth going through, I can say unequivocally that it is. The puzzle is now back together–all of my pieces are in place. It took years of courage and perseverance to accomplish this. I have come through a long, dark forest into a clearing where the sun is shining brightly.

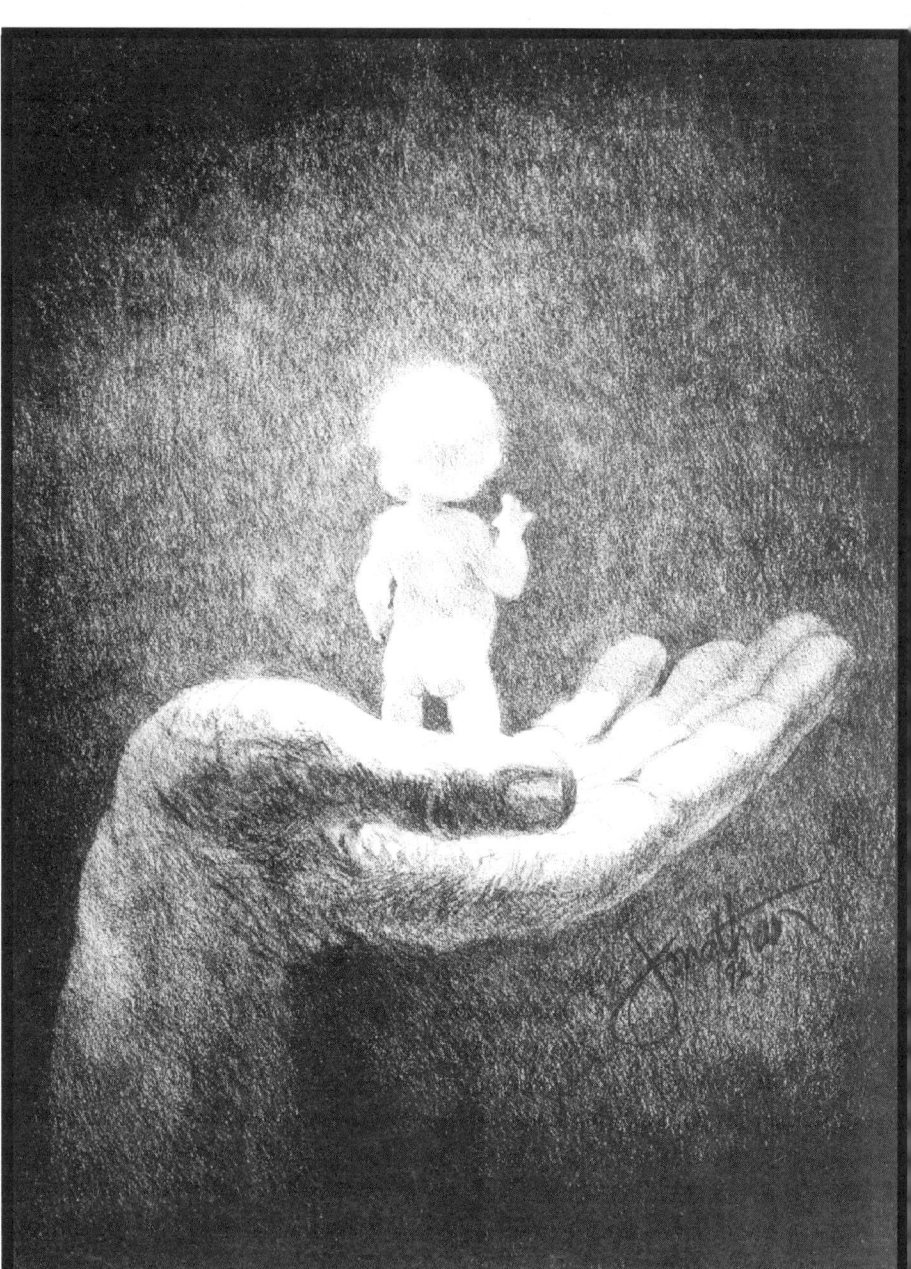

Dixie

I was born in Idaho, raised in Washington, reared a family in Texas, and am now living in San Francisco, where I have a practice in Rapid Eye Technology and other intuitive arts. My husband, Lynn, and I are devoted to the protection and uplifting of all survivors of life's harsh experiences. The following story, abridged and edited, derives from my book, Hide and Go Seek.

When my then current husband was arrested in the summer of 1979 for exposing himself to neighborhood children, my fantasy world began to crumble. However, it took three more years for me to break away from the denial cementing our relationship. After the divorce, some of our six children began to complain about feeling uncomfortable around him. I finally called Child Protective Services to check it out.

What progressed was a journey of discovery that has not yet been fully navigated. Several child specialists believed the children needed therapy and protection from their father and tried to help me get legal and psychological help for them. The ensuing years were filled with over sixty court motions, virtually all of which I handled *pro se* after we ran out of money and therefore out of attorneys.

My new husband's psychology practice was destroyed, our expensive home lost, friendships shattered and families torn apart. Even church officials deserted us as the tornado swirled.

Although we often felt a richness of divine love and direction in the midst of all the turmoil, I desperately needed what I could not buy: legal help, community support, physical health, and psychotherapy for everyone. It was indeed the best of times and the worst of times. I was finally driven to taking my youngest children underground, which lasted for three months. We were found and the children returned to their father. My husband Lynn and I spent weeks in jail pondering what had happened.

Confusion about my birth family's part turned to anger as I followed the trail of clues I was now picking out of the debris. My father finally admitted helping my ex-husband find us.

Lynn and I moved from place to place, withdrawing more from society and family. As beautiful and as peaceful as the places were that we discovered in the Northwest, grief about the children darkened the solace of our surroundings.

Stung by my father's confirmation of the family's conspiracy, I read *Toxic Parents*, by Susan Forward.[1] I began to recognize unhealthy dynamics afoot in my birth family, which my children's therapists had always questioned.

John Bradshaw's TV workshop on the inner child stirred up even more for me. I bought a notebook and hid in the fir trees around the lake near our travel trailer, determined to focus on a childhood sparse of memories. I remembered more and more—good and bad—and wrote whatever I felt. Lynn kept reminding me that this was not about blaming my parents; it was to simply allow myself to examine what I felt, "justified" or not.

In the fall of 1991, I heard from someone who remembered seeing his father knock me down as a child after I yelled that I would tell my parents what he had done to me. I was aghast. Here was the first evidence that any abuse might have occurred to me. I drove over the mountains to see him the next day, a significant reaching out after years of withdrawal. I was met with understanding beyond my hopes.

While visiting in his home, I was introduced to a counselor who used Educational Kinesiology[2] (Edu-K) to release and repattern beliefs being held in the mind. I immediately made

[1]Forward, Susan. *Toxic Parents*, New York, 1989.

[2]Edu-Kinesthetics, Ventura, California, (800) 356-2109.

an appointment. As we worked together, fleeting, indistinct visual memories stirred from their locked vaults. Emotions welled up in me as if pockets of trapped information had been waiting decades to be unlocked. I knew terrible things had occurred to my body. It was a major shake-up of my view of my history. The most charged sensation that came up for me in this initial session was the deep belief that it was dangerous to be alive. Connected to this was my long held fear of "evil spirits." By the time I left the counselor's country house, snow was falling on this dark Halloween night, and I anticipated a frightening drive through the back roads with dark spirits challenging me at every turn. Instead, I felt no fear. It was as if I could look at such ghoulishness as an observer instead of a victim.

The difference was so pronounced that after the next session I went on a victory walk, ending up at a haystack in the field neighboring my friends. I climbed to the top and looked down. Suddenly I saw an indistinct scene below of men around something. They had on different clothes and their faces were obscured. I shouted down, "You guys are just stupid men scaring little children! I'm free!!" My shout of freedom rang throughout the valley.

The puzzling events of the last few years were now suddenly making sense. I ran into other people who had grown up at about the same time, in the same place as I had, and who were either professionally or individually bumping up against similar puzzle pieces, with none of us having the complete picture. These memory puzzle pieces involved blood. They involved scenes of groups of adults hurting and "teaching" children. They involved animal abuse. They involved pain.

As we tried to figure this out, we referred to legal material and talked to knowledgeable therapists. The repeated elements seemed consistent. It looked and felt like ritual abuse.

I read *Reach for the Rainbow*[3], written by a woman who had repressed being abused by her famous father (a Hollywood screenwriter), splitting her mind in order to survive her

[3]Finney, Lynn D. *Reach for the Rainbow*. Park City, Utah, 1990.

environment. She explained Multiple Personality Disorder (MPD) as a psychological defense much more common than professionals had originally imagined. She explained that a person utilizing this defense fragments in a continuum from very slight differences or pockets, to starkly observable personalities that may not even know of one another.

Another document I found meaningful was a copy of an internal memo by a high official in my church[4], who had interviewed sixty ritual abuse survivors and who was attempting to educate the ecclesiastical hierarchy about this kind of abuse. Several parts of the memo hung in my mind.

He said that most of the survivors had developed psychological problems and most had been diagnosed as having some form of dissociative disorder or MPD. He said that the objective of ritualistic child abuse is premeditated–to systematically and methodically torture and terrorize children until they are forced to dissociate so that there is no day-to-day memory of the atrocities.

I asked my husband if in his professional opinion he saw indications that I might be multiple, and he said that he had never observed me to be losing time or consciousness, and that my Minnesota Multiphasic Inventory (MMPI) tests didn't suggest it. We later found they rarely do.

Meanwhile, I was interfacing with more hometown victims of childhood abuse. Someone asked my husband what we survivors planned to do with the information we were gathering about victims and perpetrators. He thought a minute and then answered, "They plan to heal."

Although my emotions and part of my rational mind accepted that I was treading into valid waters, there was constant internal yammering.

"How could a bunch of farmers have done anything like that? This took equipment. This took skill. This took organization."
But remember, Moses Lake was the site of perhaps the most techno-

---

[4]Memorandum dated July 19, 1990 from Bishop Glenn L. Pace to Strengthening Church Members Committee, reprinted by *Salt Lake City Messenger*. Salt Lake City, 1991.

logically advanced Air Force Base in the United States, and some people are remembering being abused there.

"You're just making this up because you're mad at your family."

And I wonder why that could be!

I couldn't answer all the inner questions. But once I started becoming aware, I asked only one thing—to be guided to truth, no matter what it was, no matter what its source, no matter where it led.

And for the strength to deal with it.

Nights were difficult. Sleep often eluded me, and dreams were disturbing. Emotions rose and fell unpredictably. Locked energy surfaced in pain as the body remembered in its own way. And always, always, there was the knifing pain of the loss of my precious children.

Nightmares arose as well. One night at my friend's home, I dreamed I was sitting in a dank, decaying Gothic structure with my dead sister Vickie. She looked beyond me, over my shoulder, and communicated the idea that she saw something I needed to see, but it would be horrible. I suddenly knew if I turned around I would see a dragon-like Satan behind me. The sheer terror awakened me. I was frantic to creep into someone else's bedroom and crawl in with them (I had come without Lynn), or to sleep on the floor, but I could not bring myself to move out of my paralysis.

Inheritance money came at the perfect time, paying for my therapy and training in Edu-K. I replenished that money by teaching Edu-K, which enabled me to have sessions and be trained in Rapid Eye Technology, a healing program developed by Ranae Johnson[5] that simulates on a more conscious level the stress-releasing eye movements of dreaming sleep. This was another miracle for me.

I used these and other methods, and practitioners, to address deep emotional and physical pain. The methods were working, not just theoretically but where it counted—in my everyday life. Nevertheless, while I was experiencing great

[5]Rapid Eye Institute, Salem, Oregon. (888) 399-1181.

changes, there were still ups and downs. I wanted to feel good every moment of every day, so I constantly sought deeper self-awareness, believing by then that all external situations were merely mirrors or messages to me of what was hidden inside myself.

Books became an additional feeding ground and I found rich fodder in diverse volumes falling (sometimes literally) into my hands: *Embraced by the Light*, by Betty J. Eadie, *Quantum Healing*, by Deepak Chopra, *People of the Lie*, by M. Scott Peck, to name a few.

In the summer of 1993, I received a call from a detective. My children's father was again under investigation for molesting more teenagers. His arrest, conviction, jailing, disbarment and second excommunication from church were almost more than I could believe after so many years.

Incredibly, however, despite all of the legal vindication given our efforts to protect the children, Child Protective Services said that to get custody while he was in jail, I would have to hire an attorney and go before the same judge who gave him the children. No attorney would even talk to me without thousands of dollars in retainer, and legal assistance efforts fell apart just as they had years earlier.

So it was a major disappointment when our hopes were dashed. But a crucial event had occurred, and I knew we were on our way out of hell.

My older estranged children and I began talking in varying degrees of openness, and in February 1995 I defied the court order denying me visitation. We all greeted each other with tears at the home of my stepdaughter.

OCTOBER 19, 1995.

A body/mind therapist pressed into a point of pain in the right side of my sacrum. I felt as though I had been suddenly dropped into another time and place.

"What is going on, Dixie?"

"Entrainment."

I didn't know what that meant even though I'd said it. The

practitioner briefly explained the phenomenon of psychological programming and then told me to relax back into the setting.

"How old are you?"

"I'm little. I'm three or four."

"Is anyone there besides you?"

I studied my mind's eye, as if looking around the room.

"Yes." *There are mean men. Their meanness is not just in what they are doing to me but that they are doing it with such detachment. I am crying from pain and from lack of caring.*

"Can you describe anyone to me?"

The one closest to me fills up most of the space. His waist and bottom area are large. The pants are khaki, the shirt is dark blue. There is a florid tie. There is a white smock. The belt. It is closer to me than anything else. It is so worn that the original brown is fading from the edges.

This man has wire-rimmed glasses. His dark hair is receding and fairly shaggy, fairly oily. There is a thin dark beard—but no mustache—over porous facial skin. The eyes are surprisingly light greenish. And distant.

I described briefly what I was seeing.

"Are these people talking to you?"

"No. But they are German. No, the one by me is Slavic, I think."

What the heck am I saying? The nationality itself was not important to me—merely the fact that I could differentiate languages. Again I asked the therapist for understanding.

"You've heard those sounds since and your internal computer can match them up, particularly if they were heard during trauma. Go back into it, Dixie. You're doing a good job. Let it come. And just tell me if it gets too rough."

I had waited forty-seven years with this festering inside me; I was not about to back off. I moved my awareness back into this scene. The pain in the sacrum helped me reenter the setting from which my body and mind had protected me for decades.

I am so little and they are so mean.

"Why are they doing this?" the therapist interrupted.

That's what they do. They don't care. They are being paid. It hurts so bad.

My mind swooshed open and I saw this whole scene from a different level.

They are scientists. They have done studies for years in prisons and hospitals. Some of the studies have never been published, and never will be. The techniques they use are very carefully guarded.

Their services are purchased. They do not live here. We seem to be in a portable laboratory. There is warm wood, like varnished pine, and there is what I will later know as stainless steel. And there is pain. My eyes fix and my breath stops and every muscle tenses to endure. And there is a point at which endurance is not possible and the mind flees.

The fiery hot pain in the sacrum had subsided. I was weeping, but it was now merely a flow that I allowed to ebb. I rested.

"Let's check the other side. Is there anything here?"

This is the secret one.

There was wailing coming from deep within. I kept crying out in anguish, "My children! My children!"

The critic finally broke through the sobs to ask why a four-year-old would be screaming out about children she had not borne.

It's about the messages, the warnings. This is where the pain is going in when they tell me if I don't obey, my babies will be taken away from me.

I suddenly realized that when I started therapy a decade earlier I had started disobeying, and that every secret cell in my body knew it. That's why every step of growth I took had been so painfully marked by fear.

"I knew. I knew what might happen ... I can't believe I actually did it! ... I actually broke out of some circle of programming they put me in! They never thought I would do it ... They knew I would never give up my children ... They knew even the church would reinforce choosing my family over my freedom. They never thought I'd do it! ... I can't believe I did it!"

I wept and wept in recognition, in horror, in amazement.

The therapist stroked my forehead.

"Freedom had a high price for you, didn't it, Dixie?"

Some hours later as I drove through the verdant landscape sliced by Highway 5 on its way to Oregon, the peace of catharsis sharpened the sunny day. Awareness after awareness flowed through me, insight after insight. I pondered how much strength of will it had taken to trade so much–church, reputation, family, friends, children. For what? For freedom from something still largely unclear to me. I thought of my mother teaching church youth in the 1960s. One morning she spun the tale of the latest dramatic escape over the Berlin Wall. She made a lasting impression on us about how the soul innately yearns for–demands–freedom.

A few miles and a few thoughts further on, a stunning truth dawned on me like a brilliant sun rising over a dark sea. I understood what had been known in a deep part of my soul–some part so deep it had surpassed the embedded memory of torture of a four-year-old girl and the unconscious threat to a terrified woman.

The only way for me to truly free my children was for me to be free first!

In November 1995, I visited a friend in southern Utah. Cara had been trained by an Arizona Rapid Eye Technician, Keith Redford, in an innovative method of identifying, processing, and integrating multiple personalities, and I was privileged to sit in on part of her work.

The next week Cara set up a booth at a convention and I accompanied her. One afternoon I overheard words drifting across the room. "Father," "government official," "World War II," "ex-Nazis," "killed him …" When I could grab the woman speaking, she briefly repeated her own family's experience, which she had chronicled in a book.[6] The fact that there were so many common elements to my memory of entrainment, was significant validation.

[6]I regret not acquiring her name or book title that day, because I didn't see her afterwards.

My husband called me that night saying we had been asked if we wanted to manage a small apartment building in San Francisco. It somehow felt right, even though we had just opened a promising practice and sorely needed dependable income. I flew home and prepared clients for our departure.

I immediately fell in love with San Francisco. We soon had clients who seemed to have been waiting for us, and that felt promising. In the summer of 1996, my husband and I called Keith Redford about his work with fragmented personalities. He confirmed that traditional testing does not often "catch" MPD; it depends on which alter is sent forward to take the MMPI, for example. He said current studies suggest that a majority of women split to some degree, which made me feel less unusual.

I asked Keith if he could tell over the phone if I had alters (as the splits are often called). He said we could try it. He asked me to breathe deeply, to relax, to notice what happened in my mind's eye or feelings when he asked me questions, and to let myself express whatever felt like coming up. When I saw a little girl peeking around a corner of my mind, he asked me to "step to the side" and let him talk to her. I took a few breaths and waited for nothing to happen. Suddenly I felt sad and scared and little and, as he talked to me, I felt like speaking in little words and a little voice. Again, as in Seattle, there seemed to be a part experiencing, a part observing, and another part criticizing the experience. Keith spoke to each of these parts in turn, and each time there was a discernible shift in my energy, thoughts, and feelings. We decided his technique might work for me.

Because of my husband's experience as a psychotherapist, Mr. Redford rapidly taught him how to work with me. My husband and I were soon sitting in the living room talking about how to approach my alters.

I suddenly started crying. My husband asked what was wrong, but I didn't know. I was as surprised as he was. We let my crying continue.

Soon my husband gently asked, "What is your name?"

"Crybaby," I heard myself say, wailing that everyone was mean to call me that. "Sometimes they call me a 'Big Boob,' or 'Baby'."

"Why do you cry?"

"Because I'm so sad, and I don't get to cry. Everybody keeps shutting me up."

I kept thinking that I needed to be taking notes, which was interruptive and annoying. I said something about it to Lynn and realized I was not feeling like a bawl-baby anymore; I was clinical and eager to have this recorded. I even felt like a male. Lynn picked this up and asked, "To whom am I speaking?"

"I'm the one who is always making notes so I can tell the story later."

They talked and when Lynn promised to take notes, there were no more interrupting thoughts. And once again, I felt like a big bawl-baby!

"Do you know that changes are going on inside Dixie, preparing for integration, where all of you will be one?"

(Crying) "*Don't you do that* unless you let me get it all out first or it's just like doing what everybody else does."

"I promise you can cry as much as you want."

I laid on the bed weeping for a long time. Eventually Lynn asked, "What's going on now?"

"No one ever asked me before how I felt. The first time was when you did, before you married Dixie. You said things like she did have sadness and that it was understandable. You stood up for me before anybody else did, even Dixie. You gave her the message to start looking for me and to take care of me."

As interesting and productive as this time was, within an hour I was feeling drained. A call to Keith Redford confirmed that many of our experiences were consistent with his own research. He said that the fatigue I felt might be due to my staying co-conscious, which takes more energy. That is, my presenting personality "listened in," and "I" could remember in different degrees of clarity what was going on no matter which alter was forward. He said that some people are totally unaware of what has transpired in session.

One way of noticing when an alter was forward in me was when I started saying "she" or "Dixie." I now realized that many of the thoughts always running through my head were voices of truly different parts of me, almost like old friends I had been pretending I did not know. Focusing on them in the driver's seat reminded me that these friends had been coming in and out of the driver's seat so smoothly I had not recognized the switching. I felt love for those parts of myself that had served so well and felt so much. "*Aha*," I might think, "*You're the one who felt childish around authority figures, right?*"

Each day we drew stick figures and labeled my alters and, as they spoke, Lynn dutifully took what notes he could. More important, Lynn and I allowed each to express and process whatever feelings he or she held, often changing their jobs or integrating "clusters" with similar functions on the same day they were discovered. Consequently, I didn't have months or years getting deeply acquainted with all the parts I had created–I continue to understand more only in retrospect. We found that some of the alters did not have feelings one way or another about things; as they repeatedly said, "It's just my job." Keith confirmed the fact that Rapid Eye processing dramatically speeds up the healing of emotion-holders, but that logic seems to convince the intellect-based alters that, while their jobs are acknowledged and appreciated, they are no longer required, and in fact may now be undermining the very person they were created to sustain.

In this manner, by the time I went to Arizona for final integration, there were far fewer voices inside, and most were encouraging.

I'd like you to meet some of the "me's" I created.
I have discussed Crybaby. Maré was discovered when Keith suggested that we look for the part most connected to God. I became relaxed and Lynn asked if such a one could come forward. I closed my eyes, took a couple of deep breaths, and, as usual waited for nothing to happen. In a few seconds,

however, I felt very peaceful, very loving.

"Hello, Lynn," I felt like saying, so I did.

"Thank you for coming forward. Can you tell me who you are?"

"You may call me Maré. You might think of me as mostly feminine. I am the healthy part that never fragments. I have helped Dixie by leading her and the whole system towards health. I direct at the soul level. I have led them through things you wouldn't believe. And I have loved Dixie even when she hated herself.

"I have been preparing alters for this process, telling them that something good is going to happen."

"Can we help you?"

"It is actually the reverse. I am in the spirit realm, but also in the body to an increasing degree." I came to understand that this was the discernible portion of my spirit, or "higher self" as some called it.

Maré became our greatest ally, as she could suggest ways of handling situations with alters which had Lynn stumped. She also occasionally made profound observations that were very illuminating to us both.

"Take in or accept only those intents or thoughts coming in on the love frequency" she once suggested. "If there is any anxiety, fear, or agitation attached, it is on a lower frequency and doesn't have to be accepted as being in your highest good. This applies to what you hear or see, including what is on TV, radio, or around other people. This is also protection against those seeking to control the world. The frequency they *cannot* access or manipulate is the love frequency."

Maré also explained that all the previous inner work I had done had been important preparation for the integration to go more quickly and smoothly, and that some alters had already integrated. Often many "copies" of an emotion-holder are created when one "part" can't take any more fear, for example. The mind creates another cubicle to handle the fear that is still being experienced. As I processed long-buried emotions, these copied parts seemed to deflate and integrate into fewer parts.

As a result, I didn't focus on how many alters I had developed, or even to what degree of split they were on the continuum, but on making sure each was ultimately honored and processed, whether separately or in a group.

Another thing I learned was that certain alters seemed to be attached to each other, almost as if they operated in clusters, or had related jobs. Other people working with alters have since described to me similar impressions.

I will give you a few highlights of others:
REPORTER:

A male, in his twenties; his job was to report what Dixie experienced. Created to try to remember and tell, he was always writing a book or taking notes. It was irritating to the other alters. This one helped me to be a better speaker and writer, which was so crucial during the years in court.

Maré commented: "The disadvantage is that constant rehearsing is like a ladder across the rich chasm of 'now,' bridging the past and future so that the present gets missed. As soon as the 'now' is experienced, he practices reporting it, and it is instantly gone. More correctly, *Dixie* is gone from *it.*"

FATIGUE:

She carried the energy of fatigue for me that permitted the rest of me to continue my drive toward perfection in the midst of such inner turmoil. "There are several, by now, who hold this in layers," she explained. "We've been filling up with fatigue for a long time—like the Painholders, since childhood. Besides performing physical activities of the body, other parts that run mental or emotional processes also create fatigue—Hypervigilance and Judgment, for example—and this fatigue is also stored here."

I found myself realizing through my own work and working with clients, that fatigue is not an absence of energy, but a particular *kind* of energy.

GUILT:

An ageless male, reddish-blackish energy, this one said, "You can call me Satan." It was his job to pass on the teachings of guilt to assure that nobody broke through to reality. He popped up whenever strong alters—especially Anger—came forward.

"This keeps them denied in expression, thereby keeping them underground, thereby keeping them intact."

He also created double binds; e.g., guilt about anger and guilt about passivity. "She's damned if she does and damned if she doesn't. I get her coming and going." A core negative belief was that *guilt is good; guilt guides one to heaven.*

The energy came in at conception, as if the very act that created me was so clouded with the guilt and shame of my parents that it permeated me immediately.

Guilt was aware of coming changes, and of changes already started. He was willing to contemplate the possibility of choosing a higher vibration, but as Lynn spoke to him about changes, he complained, "You don't seem to value me."

"That is true, I probably don't."

"You don't see my ultimate purpose."

"What is it?"

"To create a contrast so Dixie can choose consciously."

THE EVIL ONE:

This was the female counterpart of Guilt (Satan), as if two cells had not completely separated. Her job was to hold the energy of evil. "I carry the reality that Dixie is innately evil, that at the base of all reality is damnation, evil, fire, baseness.

This belief was strengthened at times of "deep, dark secrets." Although she did not reveal what that meant, images of a cave, penises, worms, and a feeling of sexual energy came up.

Maré explained further: "Her job is to create the particular clouds of energy in Dixie that certain entities can feed on. Dixie has, in that sense, been a host to parasites. This has been a very deeply hidden function so that Dixie's appearance, behavior, and awareness could belie such an existence, which keeps it safe from detection and therefore safe to continue production.

The Evil One created the basic belief that sex and sexual feelings are the deepest evil.

Maré again elucidated: "This is an understandable belief because the times in which Dixie felt the deepest evil were often when there was sexual energy around. And during even the most nurturing experiences of her family life, the subject of sex was absolutely taboo, so she didn't have a positive contrast."

FREQUENCY MODULATOR (FM):

Its job was to modulate frequency so that each cell got the right amount of electricity to perpetuate the programmed parts of the internal system that was designed by those who invested in the programming. I didn't understand and asked, "Who monitors?"

"Many. Government 'researchers,' those in black air vehicles, some nonhuman beings using 'researchers' as a front."

This answer was ridiculous to me at the time, but some pieces are coming together that indicate the government may, indeed, have been involved in my abuse.

One day while in session, I kept noticing something in my mind's eye similar to a fixed sheet of wavy glass or plastic, with what looked like the image of a young girl imbedded in the material—somewhat like a photograph. It was at first just an irritant, since I often assumed that pictures in my mind were visual trash.

Finally, however, I asked an alter we called Observer about it. Observer said it was a girl trying to be dead, to be unobserved. Observer called her "dormant." I could then see that Maré stood in front, partially to hide her from those who might disturb her prematurely, and partially to send soft rose/pink/lavender glowing from Maré's gown or aura into the "glass."

Lynn started asking for this little girl to wake up and come forward, and again I took some breaths and tried to be "blank." A change came over me as I felt anger at being disturbed. It seemed as though a great deal of the anger was due to the fact that it was disturbing a previously successful attempt to convince myself—whoever *that* was—that I was dead.

At first, I just struggled to avoid Lynn's voice and refused to talk. When that didn't work and I felt more and more alive, I began to cry.

"Leave me alone! I want to go back!" I kept repeating, turning my face from him.

It was too late. Everything I was feeling, Dixie—the more adult part of me—started speaking, betraying me further by blinking the eyes in the Rapid Eye method of processing feelings. This made me feel them even more.

"I want to go back! I don't want to be here! I can't do this. I want to be dead!"

I stopped breathing, sinking back into the warm void. I floated comfortably on and on, until Lynn desperately yelled to me, jarring me back into harsh reality.

Lynn brought Maré forward, who said we needed to proceed carefully since this one—Rose—was very fragile and had indeed been dormant for many, many years. She also confirmed our sense that there was a difference here, that this was not really an alter but the original me.

Lynn had strong emotional reactions to Rose. He firmly believed that she needed to be nourished over a long period of time to be strong enough for the final integration coming in Arizona.

At this time, four of my children were due to visit us in San Francisco—a first. We were still estranged, still trying to find out who each other was without the ability to really talk much about it. I was concerned that since I had opened up so many parts of myself, some would pop out at inopportune times. Lynn asked Maré what could be done to make the visit smooth. The first thing she said was, "Protect the baby."

"How?"

"Ask me to do it."

So he asked, and I reported that in my mind's eye I saw her put the same pastel colored lights around and through Rose, and stand guard over her.

We also agreed that Lynn should ask everybody inside to

listen up. I felt as if I suddenly had many ears as he explained the upcoming visit and asked for the cooperation of everyone. He was specific with certain ones, even asking some to baby-sit or keep those, who might be most disruptive, occupied. It seemed to work, because the visit went much better than I expected and I felt like an adult most of the time.

From then on, when Lynn wanted to work with or check on Rose, he went through Maré. She would report that Rose was being nurtured and tutored. I could not logically understand how a part of my mind could be having experiences while another part (Dixie) was unconscious not only of the experience but of its background. The whole field of the unconscious, however, is one of the nonlogical; I had learned enough to trust that powerful healing takes place there, mostly through symbols, including pictures or visualizations. I also trusted that the spirit realm was as real as the physical.

Maré would occasionally "bring out" Rose for short periods during calm parts of sessions, or when we would go on excursions that Maré suggested. We would arrive at our destination and then relax and invite Rose to be brought forward. I remember watching the clouds change forms above me as we lay on the cool grass at Golden Gate Park. I suddenly heard a voice in my head say in excited recognition, "Sheep!"

Another time in the courtyard of the nearby synagogue, my eyes lit up and I turned to Lynn, pointing.

"Bird."

That struck the adult part of me as funny and I was glad no one else was around. I felt free to watch the birds and let my hands play in the sparkling water of the fountain. It was a delightful new sensation.

Rose also enjoyed watching the ocean waves roll up on the sand at sunset. She was beginning to cry less about being here.

But she still loved to spend time with some nice ladies–angels, I think–at a place I eventually saw with her. Hollyhocks, morning glories, and her favorite flowers, roses, poked through a brown picket fence. I/she seemed to be nestled in deep moss in the crotch of a big oak tree. Intensely blue skies with puffy clouds peeked through the shady leaves. I delighted in watching birds and chipmunks playing around me. I knew I/Rose loved it here.

I described what I was seeing and feeling to Lynn. Then I started to cry. "They always make me go back!" I sobbed.

I knew I had often gone to this place of peace and beauty as a child when I was hurting too much from abuse to stay in the body. I also knew I finally couldn't take having to come back so often and was allowed to go dormant. I felt that all the others, including the Dixie seen by the public, were formed subsequent to this descent by Rose into dormancy.

It was a very tender time whenever Rose came up. I would have felt this tenderness for any child, but I knew that this was the original me, and even when I was not experiencing her forward, my heart ached with love for this precious little one. I wondered if this was the baby I was always trying to breast feed in dream after dream, night after night.

One afternoon while Rose lay on the couch listening to the hauntingly beautiful CD, *Secret Garden*, Lynn lovingly patted my arm. It seemed to hurt. I tried to ignore it but as he gently stroked me, I could not help crying, now from tension. My body seemed wracked with the memory of pain, and even his loving touch jarred it. I had to tell him to stop. As soon as he kept his hand in one place, the tension subsided and the sense of release returned, now with a deeper element of self-pity and grief.

In October 1996, we had a mass "meeting" in which Lynn asked for any alters who had not changed jobs and were ready to do so, to hold up their hands. In my mind I saw several. I relaxed and let them come up one at a time. Many clusters had integrated into one, so there were far fewer alters by now. Lynn had continually assured everyone inside as a group, and as individuals, that no one was going to die; no one was going away. This had been a concern of several alters, who often felt they might be rejected, or who didn't know how to do anything but their jobs. "You can learn many exciting ideas of new ways to serve Dixie when you are filled with light," Lynn would suggest to puzzled alters worrying about their futures.

My alters were often tired anyway, and once they processed and knew everyone would be safe without their old jobs, many came up with inventive and helpful new assignments for themselves while waiting for final integration. This is a crucial step because it literally sets new neuropathways into the mind and body.

The Critic group became The Cheerleader, encouraging me rather than finding fault. Bobby chose not to manipulate as before, but to gather and tie together pieces of information so I could heal faster. Others made similar changes, usually in direct contrast to what they had formerly done.

I did not live long in the awareness of my multiplicity. By the first week in November, I was making preparations to go to Arizona to finish the integration and take Keith Redford's training. With two days to go, I felt nervous turmoil in the ranks. My alter, Hate, came out denigrating Lynn, Keith, and myself, making fun of "love and light." We did Rapid Eye, and in the usual practice of reframing or replacing the energy, Lynn said, "Now let's blink in some good energy."

Hate was incensed. "I heard that!"

"What?"

"You said 'good energy.' You think my energy wasn't good. I can't believe *you* of all people would judge me, Lynn! I thought you understood me the most, and that's why I trusted you so much."

Lynn apologized profusely, admitting that he *had* seen hate as "bad." Hate broke down, angry over all the judgment of his energy. He was aware that he was created when Dixie expressed anger that was judged, and that thereafter had to go underground. "I've held this for her all these years, and this is the way I'm treated," he complained.

He finally settled down and finished his job change, but Lynn and I both learned much in the process.

Keith Redford picked me up at the Phoenix airport and we went directly to his office for marathon sessions before his training class would begin the next day. He found more alters connected to the "cult," although we didn't take the time to gather nonessential information on what "cult" meant. He did Rapid Eye on remaining groups of emotion-holders to make sure they were clear before integrating. He reminded everybody that no one had died, no gifts or abilities were lost; jobs were just changed and life-force shared. Pretty soon there were only two or three left, and one of them was Rose.

As Rose, I processed for hours, feeling intense emotions. Finally it was past time for a break, and when asked what she would like to do, Rose said she would like to go outside, in the nature that she loved.

Keith started for the door and, as I moved out of the chair, I bent over, trembling. I could not stand up! I crumpled onto the floor, crying, "It hurts, it hurts, it hurts."

I suddenly realized I had never walked when Rose was forward. My physical body was obviously still holding great pain energy that was stored in the body along with Rose.

Keith turned back and started spiraling the Rapid Eye wand [used in Rapid Eye therapy] over my body, telling me to "let it all come out; gather it all up and release it to the light. Let your eyes help you by blinking; just keep gathering it up and letting it go."

I don't know how long this went on but some time that evening, Rose walked for the first time in forty-seven years.

Two days later, in front of the MPD class, Rose, along with the last remaining logic-based alter and the last remaining emotion-based alter, integrated into the body, housed at that time by Maré. It was an unexpectedly stirring procedure, and when it was finished I felt "all-at-one" for the first time I could remember.

The difference I felt after integration was definite but not earthshaking, maybe because so many had begun to change through the years of therapy, and because some were so deeply hidden I hadn't consciously been aware of them until Lynn and I were taught to find them. The most notable difference has been a feeling of centeredness, of oneness, as if I'm all in one place. It seems that growth and insights are accelerating. Relationships seem to improve as I am more at peace with myself. I occasionally feel an impatience for more clarity and validation about my childhood and the people involved in it, but it is coming and I am more patient.

I gave up the need to focus on forgiveness years ago when I realized that it is a by-product of healing and can't be pushed without damage to the process. So when I notice feelings of anger, I try to accept them and process them through, listening to any direction about action that might be appropriate to help myself heal. Slumps occur, but are fewer and less intense.

Outer miracles continue to reflect inner changes. My oldest daughter married a man who not only supports her path to healing from her abuse, but is brave enough to address his own healing process. She is now a powerful therapist-in-training. My second daughter became a massage therapist too, fascinated with the diversity of body healing techniques she is gathering. She is in a loving relationship with a man of depth and sensitivity. My third daughter has moved out of her father's environment and is forging a new life for herself. My fourth child recently married, moved away, and started his own family. The fifth met a magical friend who has enabled him to feel alive emotionally. The sixth, my baby, is entering early adulthood and, as a pianist, shines with a talent so bright it promises to free her from financial dependence on the perpetrator. So the shackles are falling, just like the poignant scene in *The Temple of Doom* where the enslaved children scramble from the underground mine. My children are freeing themselves, and I am their cheerleader.

During the work with my multiples, I came to understand even more the principle of free agency. One day I realized I could no longer maintain my integrity and pay the court-controlled child support to our victimizer. It was not a matter of being naive about probable imprisonment; rather, I was willing to take whatever consequences arose. I just knew I would never again submit to him or his agents controlling me. I asked Lynn for support by not rescuing me should I be imprisoned, for I intended to be in contempt until my youngest was eighteen if necessary.

That weekend as I stood on our sailboat under the stars, I addressed the universe. I declared my intention, knowing it was honored by God. I said my preference was for this matter to be dissolved in an effortless, painless manner, with my physical freedom intact, but that regardless, my course was set and I was asking for support.

I indeed felt the whole universe shift as the scene played out without going to court, without imprisonment. On February 25, 1997, an order was signed effectively dissolving all legal connections with my ex-husband.

As he and I spoke for the first time in nine years, I told him I recognized that what he had been exhibiting in this life was not who he really is, and that I believed we had pre-mortally agreed to provide great learning experiences for one another. If so, he has certainly fulfilled his part! And I must reciprocate. I will continue to encourage—in whatever way my spirit directs—the breakdown of denial preventing this man from acknowledging he has created victims, the greatest being himself. I will continue to champion the opening of *all* secrets.

I cherish the vision I hold of all of us—individuals, families, societies—at last being truly free.

5

Susan

I have taught myself how to do desktop publishing on my computer, and like to create logos, business cards, and brochures for my friends in the alternative health field. I am working on a book of my own that I hope to publish within the next two years. I have written and facilitated workshops that I feel can provide others with healing experiences. I absolutely love life! Never did I imagine I could be this content!

In 1985, I took my son, Chris, to a therapist for what I perceived to be *his* problems. When Chris and I were in a joint therapy session, we got into such a bad fight that his therapist, Ron, said he wanted to see me separately for a while. Prior to that time, no one could reach my emotions. I had gone through over six therapists before stumbling onto Ron—the only therapist who stuck by me long enough to find out anything. It took even Ron over two years to break through my defenses.

Early in 1989, Ron asked my permission to record my sessions and share them with his consulting therapist in order to obtain a clearer understanding of how to assist my healing. Because of this second therapist's help, Ron was able to determine that we were dealing with a dissociative disorder of some kind. In February 1990, I was in the psych ward of the hospital after my fourth suicide attempt. I had been experiencing a great deal of time loss which led Ron to suspect that I had Multiple Personality Disorder (MPD). While I was in the hospital, Ron put me in hypnosis and asked if there was anyone who could explain what was going on with me. Someone answered, "NO."

Ron stopped pursuing that avenue then, but by September 1990, it became evident to him that MPD was the only diagnosis that fit. I was losing time more frequently and I noticed these times were often preceded by feelings of numbness in my face, followed by sensations similar to being on hard narcotic drugs. Although I seemed to go unconscious, my friends would tell me about all the things we had done together. Consequently, Ron put me in hypnosis and asked me again if anyone knew what was going on with me. This time his question was returned by a distinctly male voice that said, "What the fuck are you in here bothering me again for? I told you in February, NO! But you are such a fucking nosy bastard that you just can't leave well enough alone..." The voice then continued with numerous other obscenities. At the end of my session, Ron told me what had happened. When I didn't believe him, he played back the tape. I was so flooded with alien emotions that I felt as if I was going to short circuit. I demanded that he shut it off! I refused to believe that this could be happening and left his office in a state of confusion.

As time went on in therapy, I first thought there were only six alters, then twelve, then twenty-one. Ron had given me an assignment to write down what I knew about each of them, how they were created, their ages, and possibly each of their functions. When I worked on this assignment, I often lost consciousness. I was continually surprised at what I read later.

However, I had heard voices inside my head–not audible to my physical ears–ever since I could remember. I had never told anyone for fear they would think I was crazy, but there were many times when my head felt like it contained a packed coffee shop where everyone is talking at once. I couldn't tell what was being said; I just heard voices talking. The chaos was unnerving, like I couldn't escape or get any privacy. Sometimes it even felt like there was a full scale medieval battle going on inside my head, complete with clanging swords, falling horses, shouting, and painful moans from the wounded. Finding out I had MPD finally furnished me an explanation.

In November, 1990, I was registered for fall quarter at the local university. After midterms, I woke up in the hospital, having attempted suicide again. I had to withdraw from school because I couldn't get released from the hospital in time to continue. Each time I was admitted to the hospital I had to take the Minnesota Multiphasic Personality Inventory (MMPI) test. The MMPI test is almost six hundred questions long and designed to assess personality and psychological problems. My test results were always the same: "Invalid, too many conflicting answers." When I expressed my confusion and resistance to a psych nurse in the hospital, she suggested I write a letter to my alters as if they were real. She thought it would help if I left a notebook by the side of my bed and invited my alters to tell me what they thought. She said I would need to be loving and accepting in my letter because they had already been hurt enough. She also suggested that I use language a child could understand. I wrote a simple letter acknowledging their efforts in my behalf and told them I wanted to give them the love and validation they deserved. I signed, "Love, Susan." The first to write back was nine-year-old Sharon. Her little note was filled with pain and fear. Eventually I came to know twenty-six alter personalities.

The following are brief examples of some of their stories:

Baby Susan (twenty-one months) was created when mother had dad put a heavy sheet of plywood on top of the playpen, making it into a cage. When I cried to get out or get nurturing and attention, mother put her face up to the bars, screamed and struck at me through the bars. I got the message that I was bad, crying was bad, and my needs were bad. The baby had most of my natural capacity to self-nurture. I was able to numb out and hide inside my mind, but that wasn't enough to make mother stop. I had become invisible by never crying. I sensed Baby Susan was out more during times when I was trying to repress escalating needs for nurturing.

Sue (two-and-a-half years) was created when I was left at home alone with my half brother, Bob (twelve years). He took me into my parent's bedroom, put me on their bed, took my pants off and played with my vagina. I didn't understand what I was feeling, only that it made me feel icky inside. Bob told me that if I told my mother what he had done, she would know I had been bad and would tie me to my bed and hit me. Then she would let him do this to me all the time.

Sue was the family scapegoat. She was blindly obedient to her elders and had extreme family loyalty. She believed her parents were perfect and were speaking for God when they told her she was evil. She was used almost consistently over the years to internalize messages of shame from family members, regardless of what kind of abuse was involved. As a consequence, she was consumed by extreme inner torment and depression. She was out during so much of my childhood that she aged along with me until I turned twelve. She stayed eleven. I believe she stopped there because her belief system was based in Concrete-Operational Thought—a cognitive condition characteristic of children from about ages six to eleven where they can only relate to concrete ideas and facts. Sometime around puberty a child can better grasp theoretical ideas.

During my adult life, Sue was active for up to three years at a time. I feel she was the dominant personality from about June of 1986 to February of 1990. She was often triggered when I felt emotional pain. Depending on the intensity of the internal pain, she would either bang my forehead repeatedly on the wall (mother used to punish me that way), or cut my arm. Mother had convinced her that people only feel internal pain when they've been sinful and need to repent, and that repentance was impossible unless you've been punished first.

Stephanie (three years) was created when I offered to help my mother put diapers in the dryer as she took them from the wringer. Mother wasn't quite ready to load them into the dryer, so I began to explore. When I was looking inside the dryer out of curiosity, my mother grabbed me by the arm and forced me inside. She hollered at me, "You don't really want to help me! You don't care how hard I have to work with two babies in diapers! You would rather see what it is like in the dryer!" Then she shut the door and turned it on. I dissociated and Stephanie was in the dryer for me. I had no memory of her experience until late March 1991. Then I began to understand why I got a smothering feeling every time I thought I was not responding fast enough to the needs of my parents or previous husbands. I experienced this same difficulty breathing when I was co-conscious with Stephanie.

Courtney (five years) came into being when my mother made me lie down on the cold tile bathroom floor, roughly pulled my pants down and told me to lie there while she prepared an enema. She kept telling me with a wicked, vicious whisper that maybe this would clean the evil out of me. I checked out when mother pushed the water in. Courtney said that the water was very hot and burned inside. Then Mother made me get up and sit on the toilet. She said the water had to be held inside for a long time to burn and clean out all the evil. She threatened punishment if I didn't hold the water long enough. Courtney tried to hold the water in, but her stomach hurt so badly that she couldn't. She said that mother pulled her off the toilet, dumped her on the floor, squatted over her, and urinated on her. Mother said, "If you don't care about getting the filth cleaned out of you, you should be filthy on the outside, too!"

This happened repeatedly over the next four years, so Courtney aged along with me until we were nine years old. Sometimes she would be able to hold the enema long enough to avoid being punished. Each time mother urinated on her, she would go hide in her inner closet before I would get to take a bath; consequently, she always felt sticky, dirty, and smelly. Courtney said that when our body was nine, mother began doing this every day, sometimes more than once a day. She got so sick that she couldn't lift her head off the pillow. Mother had been telling Dad that I had the flu so she wouldn't have to take me to the doctor, but finally Dad insisted.

The doctor took one look at me and sent my parents out of the room. He asked Courtney (assuming it was me, Susan) if she knew why she was so sick. He said he could find no reason for her to be dehydrated. (Courtney couldn't remember that word. When she shared this story, she told me that all the water was out of her body.) She told the doctor what mother was doing and told him she would be punished if mother knew she told. He called my parents back into the room and told them that he could tell by examining me that I had been given enemas and he wanted to know who was doing that and why. Mother tried to say that she had to do it because I was always constipated and was getting stomachaches. The doctor told her that he didn't believe her, but that he wouldn't report her for child abuse if she would stop without an order from him. Mother stopped.

Andrea (five years) was created when my half brother, Bob, took me into his room. I dissociated before we got there. He covered my eyes and attempted to force oral sex. Andrea managed to keep her mouth shut so tightly that he was unable to force her. Andrea didn't come up often or stay long until I was married to my current husband, Jason. When I felt her presence, it was almost impossible to respond to anyone. Sometimes my vision darkened, making it difficult to see. I sensed her presence with the other inside young ones.

Karen (seven-and-a-half years) was created one day when mother left me home alone. My half brother, Bob, entered my room. He raped me vaginally and kept saying, "Get used to it. All you get in this world is pain." Karen couldn't see what he was doing because he pushed her head toward the wall. She remembered the wallpaper and the physical pain very distinctly. I don't get a sense that Karen was out much. She was afraid of pain and sometimes came out when one of my alters was hurting the body. A few times she managed to call for help.

Sheila (seven-and-a-half years) was created during the same incident that created Karen, but Sheila experienced the sexual aspect of it. She seemed to have been created to turn the pain into pleasure. She liked rough, aggressive sex and was used several times over the years to deal with rapes and other painful sexual experiences. Sheila helped me survive several incidents of violent sexual abuse when my first husband, Gene, was drunk, so she aged with me until I left him when I was thirty-two.

Sarah (eight years) was created when mother put my hand into the wringer of our old wringer-washer. I checked out as soon as my mother grabbed my hand. Sarah despised my mother and saw her as an underhanded liar who hated children. I believe Sarah was out more during my child and teenage years. I experienced strong feelings of distaste and repulsion for my mother when Sarah was present. Sarah turned to her intellect as a way to live in a world that could not be understood. She used to hide behind a large chair in the living room and read encyclopedias.

Breezy (eight-and-a-half years) was created when Bob took me to his friend's house where he and two of his friends raped me. Breezy didn't have a name until she was eighteen and was used again during my hippie days. I needed her because I felt a strong inner aversion to the "free love" that was being pushed at the time. I have some memories that indicate that I was probably involved in sexual acts with about four hundred different boys and men over the summer of 1970. I felt light-headed and "high" when I was co-conscious with her. She stopped aging when I was twenty and quit drugs.

Brandon's characteristic "toughness" and boy-like tendencies appeared in me when I was about six years old and started school. Since my parents told me I was responsible for the safety of my younger sisters and brother in all situations outside our home, I learned to fight. Brandon did not split off and become a separate personality until I was nine-and-a-half years old. He was thirteen. My father saw me playing Tarzan without a shirt on. I was told I was too old to go outside without a shirt anymore. He carried me downstairs, threw me onto my bed, left the room and returned holding a three foot long wooden dowel. At that point I left my body and put my conscious awareness inside the wall where it was dark, safe, and nobody could get me. Brandon said he was created to "stay there and tough it out." He would always come out to take the pain of the physical beatings, and had most of the anger that naturally follows feeling powerless. He thought he should have been able to prevent or stop the beatings.

Brat (ten-and-a-half years) split off when I tried to run away and was caught. My grandmother hauled me into the house by my ear. My father snatched a hammer from the shelf, grabbed me by the arm and dragged me down the stairs. He threw me onto my bed and slammed the door. He then nailed my windows shut. When he was finished, he turned around and came toward me. When I got this memory I was unable to remember what happened next, even in hypnosis—it just went black. Brat didn't remember either; no one did. I know that I was in a great deal of pain, and that Dad locked me in my room for the following three days. Like an animal, I was brought food and water, and let out to the toilet twice daily. When Brat was out, that's exactly how I felt—like a caged animal. She housed a large amount of anger, but was easily intimidated and unable to express it, so she became passive-aggressive. She bit her fingernails rather viciously, and her anger was sometimes expressed in more self-destructive ways.

Stacey (fifteen-and-a-half years) was created when I got home from school thirty minutes late because a popular girl had spoken to me. Since I didn't have many friends, I thought it was worth getting in trouble over. My father picked up a large rock and told me he was going to show me that I belonged to him. At that point I felt as though I was sitting on the roof of the house, unable to see what went on below. He then killed my pet cat, Amber. As he was telling me I had better learn to obey his rules to the letter, Stacey showed up. She had no feelings about the value of life, nor any love for the animal my father killed in front of me. Her only thoughts were of the revenge she would someday have by killing something my father loved. Stacey was responsible for many of my previous suicide attempts.

Jamie (fifteen-and-a-half years) was created by the same incident as Stacey, but Jamie had all the feelings about her pet, as well as the resulting emotional pain of the loss. She felt she caused the cat to die because she loved it. She believed that she was a curse to every living thing that she cared about; consequently, she was afraid of getting close to anyone. Jamie was nineteen when I found out about her. She blamed herself for the drug related deaths of many of my friends while I was a hippie.

Joan Newman (fifteen-and-a-half years) was created by the same incident as Stacey and Jamie, but Joan had all the anger that I should have felt. She believed that it was Jamie's and my fault that dad killed her pet cat. She even blamed me when my ex-husband, Gene (Chris's father), committed suicide in July of 1987. She stopped aging at thirty-five, the age I was when Gene died.

Sharky (eighteen years) was created when I got caught up in a gang-type fight and ended up cutting open a girl's chest with my hunting knife. I was shocked and horrified by what I had done. The other girls pulled me into the car and sped away. They called me "The Shark," because of the way I had torn into her. I had to dissociate. Sharky came up to take pride in what I had done. She was tough. When I was upset by this recollection, she threatened me by note telling me to stay out of her memories.

Bethany Ann (eighteen-and-a-half years) was created when I met and was infatuated by a man nicknamed Smokey. I had been afraid of drugs and sex. Like everyone before him, Smokey made me feel that his happiness and his acceptance of me depended entirely upon my doing what he wanted me to do. I worshipped him and felt I could not live without him. He was continually asking me to do things that frightened me or felt bad. In 1970, I took just about every kind of street drug available, was homeless and panhandled on the streets downtown. In addition, I had about every kind of sex with hundreds of men. I hitchhiked across country, pushed drugs, had sex with policemen to keep them from arresting Smokey, ran from the cops, and spent time in jail.

Bethany Ann was out frequently after her creation. She was the benevolent and gracious granter of any wish or desire—expressed or unexpressed—of any male person I cared for from then on. She was there to be happy, no matter what. Since I was exceedingly codependent with men, including my son,

Chris, she aged until he left home when I was thirty-eight.

The last personality to form was nameless (thirty-eight years). I called her the "mom person." She dealt with the extreme feelings of shame and self-blame I experienced after August of 1989 when Chris and I decided that it would be best for him to live with his uncle. I had felt Chris needed a more stable environment than we'd had since I became so depressed and self-destructive. She believed wholeheartedly that she was the worst mother in the world and that *everything* bad in Chris's life was directly her fault. About two months after Chris moved out, my pain became too intense to bear. I had to dissociate from it; that is when the "mom person" was created. She was always self-destructive or suicidal, and her emotional pain tended to trigger Sue and Jamie.

On April 6, 1991, I gained the memories regarding what my stepbrother, Bob, had done. I had three teenage personalities, and the "mom person," who were sick of the pain. They had spent two months waiting for an opportunity to get me out of the way so they could kill the body. I had been given a prescription for Xanax to help control the shifting; however, somehow between hospital visits and new shrinks who were unfamiliar with me, these four personalities were able to stockpile the pills. Although I did not feel as if I was part of the planning, I didn't attempt to stop the process. That day, they succeeded in driving to a park where they sat in the car and swallowed thirty-seven mg. of Xanax with a pint of whiskey.

According to reliable sources, I was found almost six hours later by a policeman and had stopped breathing while he was calling an ambulance. They worked on me for about four hours in the emergency room, and then I was sent to the intensive care unit (ICU) where my body stayed on life support until April 9. I was not conscious of anything that had happened. Upon returning to life, and over the ensuing days and weeks, I had memories of my near-death experience (NDE).

The first thing I remember was being held in the arms of Jesus and the two of us walking hand in hand, communicating with each other about what had transpired. It was not verbal, or even mental. It was as though we were one person, knowing and experiencing all that we both knew and felt. It seemed I had been permeated by a sustaining love that allowed no room for shame or fear. I was freed by a boundless joy that left no residue of sorrow or pain. I was possessed by a knowing of all that is that left me awestruck with who I am. For what seemed like years, we walked and sat, held and laughed, and knew each other and all of life.

The setting was one of beautiful, immaculate grounds on the most exquisite campus! This campus could not be mistaken for one of secular learning—everything about it emanated spiritual light and knowledge. I recognized this place from previous out-of-body experiences I'd had. Later, in 1993, I began reading some books on NDEs and found a description of a similar campus-type setting in *Return from Tomorrow*, by Dr. George Richie.

During my NDE, I was given complete choice as to whether or not to return to this earth or life. I was being given information and experience to assist me in making that choice a more conscious one. Throughout my stay, I continued to choose to remain where I was. Although I was currently experiencing a complete lack of any unpleasantness, I remembered the pain I felt on earth all too well. Towards the end of my NDE, Jesus led me to an iridescent bench under a grand tree, inviting me to be with someone else. Until that time, I had only communicated with Jesus. The next instant I was sitting beside Gene, Chris's dad, who had committed suicide several years earlier.

In my heart, I had been hanging on to the thought that maybe Gene and I would be together again in another life. Gene was radiant! He held me for a long time as we shared a replay of our lives together. He told me that our intimate relationship had not been meant to last forever. A miniature holographic image appeared before me as he showed me the man I was to partner with. He told me the man's name was Jason, that he was very near to entering my life, and that he would also take his own life should I not return. There was no blame, I was simply being shown all the probabilities of my choosing. I was told that Jason had 2,341 personalities, but was not yet aware of them. I was also shown several instances in his childhood that I recognized as Satanic Ritual Abuse (SRA). This vision was the reason I chose to return

For some reason, after this experience I was able to keep from shifting again. I could hear my alters talking inside, and I could feel their desires to come out, but I did not lose consciousness again. Although my experience on the other side did not cause my integration, it did provide me some control in my life.

Prior to my NDE, I had defined myself externally—I was Chris's mom; I had a certain life-style and income level; I was Gene's ex-wife. When my son went to live with his uncle, everything I had used for self-definition was gone. This caused me to lose my sense of "I am." However, all my personalities inside had a strong sense of identity which had made them more able to take control.

After my NDE, I gained an "I am," an inside definition of myself, and a sense of my true value. I realized that I was loved, which gave me an "I" who was inherently lovable! There was now an "I" who was worth expending energy on. Before this, I shifted constantly. I was rarely present and had no way to stop the others from coming out if they wanted to. Now, because my consciousness had become strong, I could stop them. When one pressured me, I would simply explain that I needed to maintain control of the conscious mind in order to know what it was like.

It had now become important for me to protect these inside children who had had to live through horrible situations that children should never be subjected to. So now I was going to learn how to take care of things. I told them, "I need your input because you're important to me. I want to heal and I want you to heal. I want you to be loved and I want to be loved." There was no more shifting, although I heard them in my head and felt them in my heart. I was being fed new perspectives when I needed them. In a sense, an integration was happening as we were beginning to cooperate, even though we were all still separate. To me, this is what integration is—a journey toward becoming "of one mind."

Although four of the others continued in suicidal ideation, four out of twenty-six was nothing compared to the way it had been. Even without complete cooperation from everyone, I was now able to say, "No." I quit smoking cigarettes on May 3, because I was in control. There were no more feelings of numbness or being drugged. When my alters would start pressuring me, I was able to stay alert. However, sometimes the pressure would give me a headache. I would first feel a pressure or a push from inside; then it would manifest physically. Sometimes I'd actually hear them yelling at me to let them out.

The July 4th weekend 1991, was the fourth anniversary of Gene's suicide. He had shot himself in the head on July 2, 1987, but wasn't pronounced dead until the next day. Chris and I received the news upon our return from a camping trip with friends. Ron knew this anniversary was a potential bombshell so, even though he was on vacation, he set up a time for me to come in to see him. My appointment was early because he had the day planned with his family. On July 2, I had a rough time staying in charge. The grief over Gene's death belonged to me, as well as to several of the others, and it began to overwhelm me. The only thing that kept me going was knowing I had an appointment with Ron.

The morning of July 4th the alarm did not wake me; however, it did wake Joan. She turned it off and went back to sleep. Joan was one who had remained suicidal and was loyal to Gene. She didn't believe in my NDE and wanted to die to be with him. She was hoping she could gain control so she could commit suicide in the same mountains where Gene's ashes had been scattered.

When I finally woke up, the session should have been ending. I called Ron in a panic, asking if there was any way he could see me. Gently he told me there was no way he could see me until after his vacation that ended a few days later. All of my inside kids panicked because they figured everything would become out of control like before. Though Ron had helped Sue begin to understand that she did not need to be punished, she was now freaking out. In her mind, Ron had promised that he would see us that day, so she argued with him on the phone about it. Joan laid low, not letting anybody know she had a plan. I don't know how many times I shifted that morning, but I definitely was no longer in control.

Apparently Joan said good-bye to my roommate, Dana, in a way that made her suspicious. After Joan left, Dana called Ron and he called the police. A few hours later, as Joan was driving toward the mountains, she was pulled over by the police. She was trying to act like there was no problem. "My roommate is crazy. She's the one who is suicidal. Didn't you see the scars all over her arms and legs?" They didn't buy it and I was taken to the police station.

After I was released, I started back to Adult Children in Recovery meetings. I had a friend there, George, who didn't come very often, but over time we had become good friends. Our relationship was very healing for me. We talked until all hours. He had also been wounded and understood about MPD. He was bisexual when we met, but had made the decision to be strictly gay. Although our relationship was never sexual, I had spent some time imagining what it would be like to be involved. I gave up on the possibility of marriage to him; instead, we were highly intimate on a spiritual, mental, and emotional level.

One night we watched the movie *Brother Sun and Sister Moon,* about St. Francis of Assisi. After the film, we talked for hours, the conversation being spiritual and powerful. At one point, I felt Brandon look at me like he was peering from within. He just smiled and told me that I didn't need him to be separate anymore. He said I didn't need a protector—it was time for us to become one. It felt like he sat down inside me and then I had an adrenaline-like rush. After he merged, the first thing I noticed was an interest in overhead cam engines!? A sense of solidity came with the merger, a feeling of soft strength. I had a sense of having boundaries, along with the ability to maintain the boundaries—something I had never experienced before. It was awesome! I told George what had happened and we shared my joy.

In mid July, I began making more connections with another male friend, Jason, after he attempted suicide. It never occurred to me that he could be the Jason I had been shown in my NDE. He had some similar features, but wasn't nearly as attractive as the other man. I helped him decide to enter a psych hospital and gave him as much support as I could without becoming a rescuer. After ten days in the hospital, Jason told me he was getting a divorce. I felt nervous and decided that I should draw even stronger boundaries with him. I chose July 20th—at the end of a hospital visit with him—to tell Jason that I could not be more than a friend, and that I wanted to be sure he was clear about that. He told me he appreciated my honesty, and I figured that was that.

That night, I went to a friend's house. As we were talking, I received a message inside my entire body. Since my NDE, I had come to recognize these as spiritual communications. This message said, "He is the Jason you know of, your forever partner. Call and tell him." I argued with this message internally for at least ten minutes. Once again I was told, "He's the one you are here to be with."

As though in a trance, I walked over to pick up the phone and dialed the hospital. When I noticed I had dialed the number and the phone was ringing, I felt faint. I glanced at the clock. It read 10:05 P.M. I felt relieved because I knew they would not let him come to the phone. When a woman answered, I apologized for calling so late and quickly offered to call back the next day. She assured me it was okay, that Jason had been trying to reach me. When he came to the phone, I stammered, "I … I … I have something to tell you." He said, "I know, I know, isn't it neat? I received the same message! I've been trying to call you for ten minutes and you weren't home." He had been told the same thing, at the same time that I was being told. As we talked, we discovered that we both had been shown the same pictures of our future. The whole time we were talking, there was this love that was building up inside me for him, as if somebody had put it there. I had never felt anything like this before!

The next morning I met Jason at the zoo where the hospital staff had taken the patients for an outing. He told me he thought it was pretty funny that the "zoo" had taken him to the zoo. That is when we did some major falling in love; it was magical! I told him about the trouble I was having because of the four personalities that were still suicidal. I had not been able to keep from shifting since the July 4th weekend; when their feelings got strong it was difficult. I was scared because my therapist had not been able to get a contract from my personalities not to hurt the body. The only contract that he was able to get was one that we had made for that particular weekend. I was worried about what would happen after the weekend and I wanted Jason to know that he was with an irrational person. I felt that my struggles would likely affect our relationship.

Jason placed his hands on either side of my face and addressed all of us. That was the first time, EVER, that I felt all of me present at once! He spoke of his love for us with his words and his life energy. He promised that he would never, ever, hurt any of us. He said that he was extremely concerned that some of us still felt suicidal, and pleaded for a promise never to hurt my body. In return, he would give us all the time we needed to prove his promise. We all promised him! I could hear the voices from within. I was amazed that he knew enough to speak to us that way. He had no idea then that he was also MPD, and I was sworn to secrecy. He would have to discover his system and memories in his own way and his own time.

After he talked to us a little more, he said that he wanted to make things official. He asked, "When my divorce is final, will you marry me?" I said, "Yes." It seemed so natural that I didn't feel the full impact until I was driving away from the zoo and came to the first stop light. I thought, "Oh, my God, I'm engaged. What have I done?" Then a calm and a joy came over me. Every time I would start to feel scared, it was like God came and put His arm around me.

Jason had a day pass from the hospital the following Saturday, and a friend of his needed a ride to Reno, so we took him. On the way back, Jason told me about some of his spiritual experiences. As he spoke, I was visually shown what he had experienced. Even though I was driving, I saw his experiences and connected with them. He told me he had seen Christ return, dead bodies rise up, and the world turn green again where it had been decimated. As I watched the vision of this, I felt twelve of my personalities—hard core ones, like Joan and the teenagers—line up behind me in a V, like geese when they fly, and then walk into me, one right after the other. It was a strange feeling, almost orgasmic. I was filled with thoughts of gratitude and feelings of wonderment. I believe these were thoughts that had come to them since hearing Jason's experience. I was unaware of exactly who the twelve were, but I knew we had experienced a healing. I felt brand new. At my next session with Ron, he put me in hypnosis and I was able to check inside to see who was missing.

When Jason was dismissed from the hospital on July 29, he came to live with me. Within a month, some of his alter personalities came out and told me their horror stories. I helped him decide to seek therapy because I knew his healing would be far more than I could deal with alone. Although he didn't trust anyone, he agreed to see Ron, my therapist, because of what Ron had done for me. Jason remained unaware of his Satanic Ritual Abuse until April of 1992.

Because Jason began to get personally attached to my inside children, he made an agreement with each of them to tell him good-bye if they chose to merge. Once Jamie came out while I was cutting Jason's hair. She gave him such a buzz job that there wasn't enough hair left to part. She was scared, but Jason did not get angry. He held her and laughed, saying, "Now I don't have to comb my hair. Thank you." Jamie was afraid that if she loved anyone, they would die. One of Jason's personalities, J.R., looked at her belief as a challenge. He made love to her, and he did not die. The two of them became very close over time, and he still did not die. As a result, her need to stop us from loving anybody dissolved, along with the need to keep people from loving her. She no longer felt responsible for life and death.

Jamie came out one July day in 1992 and gave J.R. the most wonderful hug and kiss. He held her and then she said, "See you later, tough guy." She closed her eyes and when they opened, J.R. could see that she had become part of me. Jason told me there was a more energetic shine to my aura than before.

That autumn, my parents moved from my childhood house. Suddenly, I seemed unable to focus or ground myself, as this development threw my system into chaos. At my next session, Ron asked me where my personalities lived when they were not out. It hit me that they still lived below the basement of my parent's home. I was disconcerted by the move because all of my inner people were still under the basement. Ron and I devised a way for them to feel safe in moving out and coming with me. I placed a mental classified ad asking for their help in designing and building our dream home. The building didn't start right away, but over the next several weeks I could close my eyes and see it progress. I felt more and more connected with my selves.

In this inside dream home, everyone had a bedroom of their own. When I had first found Courtney, she was hiding in a closet. However, after Jason proposed at the zoo, Courtney put a window in the closet door, allowing her to have a real bedroom. She would often come out, Jason would hold her, and she would talk about the things she remembered had happened to her. She was afraid Jason would beat her, hurt her or punish her in some way. All Jason ever did was hold her and tell her that he loved her and that she was the sweetest Courtney he ever knew. One day Courtney came out to see Jason and told him she wanted to try merging for a few minutes. Jason said he would be thrilled to wait for her, if that's what she wanted him to do. She said it was. As Jason was holding her, she went inside, the body went limp for a minute, then came back to life. Courtney looked at Jason again and said, "It's okay, I'm going to go inside and be Susan." Jason cried and said he would miss her dearly, but would look forward to seeing her on the flip side after she was part of me. He told her he knew that she would be happier than she had ever been in her life.

Sarah was intelligent, logical, thoughtful and unemotional. She came to Jason one day and said, "You know, when somebody goes inside Susan for good, their room becomes part of the house. It's time for my room to become part of the house." That was Sarah's good-bye.

Stephanie came out later that afternoon to tell Jason that Sarah's room was part of a big indoor garden. She was upset because she was going to miss Sarah. Jason told her that she would not have to miss Sarah, that she was not gone, she was just in a different place. Jason told her if she sat still just for a second, with her eyes closed picturing Sarah, she could talk to Sarah even though she was one with Susan now. Stephanie quietly closed her eyes and was still for several minutes. Suddenly, she opened her eyes and excitedly told Jason that it worked, that she had talked to Sarah and that Sarah was happy and would always be there for Stephanie to talk to.

Andrea, my little catatonic, was next. When Jason saw her the first several times, she would sit with a blank stare, saying nothing. She could be led around; she wouldn't resist, but neither would she respond. This little one touched Jason's heart. Jason was determined to talk with her, believing in his heart that some part of her would hear him. He told her how precious she was and how much he loved her. It didn't matter to him that she didn't respond; he would talk to her anyway. Over time, Andrea did respond to him. In fact, she became quite a chatterbox.

On a spring day in 1993, Andrea was talking to Jason on the sofa in the front room when she told him she had nothing more to say, that it was time to do something different: she wanted to grow up. She wanted to be with Sarah, Courtney and Jamie. He took Andrea's hands in his, looked into her eyes and said, "I love you precious Andrea." She said, "I know Dad, I love you too." She smiled and kissed Jason on the cheek and merged with me.

Little Stephanie loved Twinkies. Jason always had a special box just for her. Stephanie taught Jason that the cake had to be eaten last, usually with half a glass of milk. When they shared Twinkies, they stuck their fingers in the middle and licked the cream off, all the while laughing and giggling. The day came when Stephanie came to Jason and said, "This is the last Twinkie, Dad." Jason replied, "Don't worry about it sweetheart, we'll buy more." She said, "No Dad, this is the last Twinkie." She poked her finger into the middle of the cream and stuck it in Jason's mouth. When she pulled her finger out of Jason's mouth, she merged. I sat there with the silliest look on my face.

Sue was the last to merge. She was the eleven-year-old who believed that her biological parents were perfect and that she was bad, evil, and terrible. Jason never argued with that. What he focused on was his experience of her. He found her delightful, precious, and beautiful—a wonderful and intelligent child of God. For the longest time, she couldn't believe Jason could love her, or that anyone could love her. There had been times when she had asked Jason to let her out of the contract to not hurt the body. Of course he wouldn't. Since she was extremely ethical and moral, she did not break her contract. With Jason's love and acceptance, Sue grew up to age thirteen.

As Sue got closer to merging, she came to see Jason quite often. After Christmas, 1993, Jason knew things had changed when she said, "Dad!" He looked at her with shock and surprise. He was so happy; he knew that her calling him Dad was a significant step. She said, "I believe you."

Jason told her he had never lied to her.

"My parents weren't perfect, were they?"

"They did the best they knew how. It was just hard for them; they didn't know what to do, especially your poor mama."

"I think I understand now. It's time for me to be with Courtney and Sarah. They need me and miss me. I'll miss you, Daddy."

"When you go in, turn around and look outside your eyes. You'll see me and I'll see you. We'll never be apart; it's just going to be different."

So she did. And so it was, and so it is.

I was unaware of Sue's integration, other than what Jason told me about it. I had never been able to be consistently co-conscious. When I was not co-conscious with the one who was out, it was pretty much like being asleep. Sometimes I would get bits and pieces of what had gone on—much like remembering parts of a dream. When I returned ("woke up") after Sue merged, I was left with a strange feeling of completeness and loneliness at the same time. It felt as if my friends had all moved away and left me on my own. Sue had liked cinnamon bears and I occasionally found that I had unconsciously bought some.

For about six months after integration, whenever I encoun tered difficult situations—the kind that elicited the feelings my alters used to hold for me, I would feel a pulling, almost a tearing inside, as if I were going to fragment again. In therapy, we worked on identifying all the various feelings I was not used to having. I learned new coping skills so I would not split off again. Ron told me there was a difference between integration (his word for merging) and fusion. He said that integration was the process of coming together, but that splitting was still a pos-sibility. He described fusion as the state of wholeness where the alters would be fused together as one, leaving separation far less likely—kind of like being welded back together.

Throughout my healing process, as well as the experience of assisting in Jason's healing, I have come to take issue with some of the "professional" viewpoints of MPD.

I believe in the beginning I was whole, precious, and fragile, and that with the abuse, natural dissociative splitting occurred. I needed to be loved, fed, bathed, protected, and marked "HANDLE WITH CARE!" I compare it to a holographic plate (a plate that holds a holographic image). As long as it is cared for, cleaned and protected, it will produce a beautiful, clear holographic image of the person within it. If someone were to hit it with a hammer, abuse it, we could not pick up the largest piece and say, "This piece could not deal with being hit, so it created all these other pieces!" It was the *abuse* that *caused* the separation, not the plate! Something interesting about holographic plates is that when they're broken, each resulting piece contains the entire original image! Each image is more faint, less defined, but has the capability of growth and change. That is how I believe alters are formed. In this sense, the host or hostess personality is just as much an alter as are the others.

I had some experiences where the beliefs and attitudes of some my friends (and, at times, my therapist) created roadblocks to my integration. Some of my alters felt like they were being asked to give up their life, free will, and identity to join with me (my host personality at the time). They got the idea that I had created them to take my pain because I was too weak to deal with it myself. This thought caused them to blame me for all their struggles, so they fought even harder against any efforts toward integration.

In addition, the "professional distance" Ron had been taught to maintain left me unwilling to open up to him much of the time; some of my alters felt like he really didn't care. I learned that love is not the same as the emotional enmeshment that "professional distancing" is attempting to avoid. On the contrary, I see love as the only true healer, and feel that a natural human can love someone dearly while staying detached from the ultimate outcome of their caring. (I did not say the "normal" human, because "normal" to me is dysfunctional.) I believe that integration is a spiritual process and that all integration is brought about by an experience of pure, unconditional love. I felt my integration progressed much more rapidly as Ron extended more love and acceptance toward me; it freed me to accept, know, and love myself. In my mind, what made Ron such a good therapist was his willingness to learn and grow alongside me. He never held himself out as a "know it all."

Although my process brought me to fusion, I'm not convinced that it is a precondition to a balanced, healthy, joyful life. I have come to see integration as a *process* of "coming together" that precedes, but doesn't necessarily have to result in, a merger or fusion. Cooperation, community, self (or selves) acceptance, "becoming of one mind," these are the types of conditions that I feel lead to health and well-being. As long as an alter personality is willing to learn, grow, and work with the others, the multiple can become fully functional without merging, if that is what they desire. Each person's system and healing process is different.

Since becoming an SPD (Single Personality Disorder), I have tried many natural alternatives for controlling my chemical depression, but it has proved most effective to keep taking antidepressants. I feel this may be due to the excessive drug abuse in my late teens, and/or the number of overdoses between 1989 and 1991. I can still get overwhelmed by chaos, clutter, or too many details; however, I am much better at noticing it early so I can center myself. I also find that it is becoming easier to accept these things about myself, and that the more I accept them, the less grief they cause. I am far less codependent and take better care of myself.

I don't think about having been a multiple anymore. I even forget about the scars on my arm for months at a time. As I continue working on myself, everything about life, joyous or painful, is a spiritual experience to me. During my NDE, I was told that there is no judgment among truly spiritual beings—there is only LOVE. That is why I now stay away from organized religion, as I have yet to find one that does not promote the "us vs. them" mind set. The more I exercise and expand my ability to unconditionally love, the more I see that forgiveness is merely a natural by-product of it. Now the greatest effort lies in overcoming the programming from abuse, and learning self love and acceptance. When this is done, all else falls into place. I believe that judgment is created by humans because they live in a world where everything is relative to something else. As far as humanly possible, I practice making continual conscious choices not to judge *anyone*–this includes the perpetrators in the world. But first, I had to remember and have a full experience of the anger that resulted from their abuse of me. It has taken me years to learn to appreciate my past as the process that lead me to remember *who I really am.*

I still get memories but, surprisingly, most of them are good now. When bad memories do come, they don't hurt as badly as before. For example, in August of 1998, I remembered what had happened after Dad came towards me with the hammer (referring to the experience that created Brat). The memory was mostly pictures—there was no longer the sting there once had been. I believe it's because most of the time now, I am able to make my own choices about what to think, feel, say, and do in my life. I choose to live from a space of LOVE, not a space of FEAR.

Otherwise, I am thoroughly enjoying my seven year relationship with my husband Jason. He continues to teach me how to see, even though he is one hundred percent physically blind. I am now completely comfortable with my sexuality. I am learning to allow myself to do more of the things I enjoy, such as playing acoustical guitar and singing, drawing pencil portraits of children, and taking long, hot baths with a good book. I work on my own, preferring not to work for someone else; it just doesn't fit who I am anymore.

There is no doubt in my mind that there is a Creator, but not one who is anything like what I was taught. I am entitled to personal two-way communication with this Being, regardless of how I choose to label Who or What It is. I know now that I am precious and beautiful—as I believe we all are. I believe it is crucial that we learn to love ourselves because all human beings are extremely precious.

6

Carol

I have a degree in psychology, and am a certified Hypnotherapist, a Master Rapid Eye Technician, and a Reiki Master. I have worked as a psychologist in Arizona for four years. I have also presented seminars and guest lectures at colleges and high schools in Arizona and Nevada on Multiple Personality Disorder. At the present time, I am co-owner of a holistic healing center in Orem, Utah.

As I ponder who I am, my strongest impression is that I am a blessed daughter of a loving Heavenly Father and Mother. I was graced with the incredible gift of dissociation. God knew I would need it to survive the traumas and abuse that would possibly come in my life. I don't believe I chose to be abused like I was, but I did choose my mission in life: to break generational abuse patterns. I did not always feel this way, but after working through my anger toward God, I realized that he did not abandon me during my abuse. There were several times that I remember being held and comforted by invisible arms. It is because of my abuse and healing that I am now able to relate to other survivors and witness their miracles in healing. I have chosen to empower survivors by assisting them in knowing and finding their own innate goodness and worth.

I was born in Utah and raised in Utah, Wyoming, and California. I lived in a home with little affection and nurturing. My mother had rigid ideas of how things should be. My father left the family when I was almost eight and within a few years my mother remarried; Mel was a sadistic, abusive man. Despite my fragmented, brutal childhood, prior to 1987 I had no indications that I was coping as a multiple. I never lost large amounts of time and I always functioned highly.

After graduating from high school, I attended California Polytechnic University with a Fashion Design and Textile major. In the summer of my sophomore year of college I had the opportunity to live with my father and his new family in Utah. I will always cherish that nine months of getting to know my father. It was during this time that my father first told me he loved me. Because he was a man of few words, I remember that moment as if it happened yesterday.

Upon returning to California, I met and married my husband, Ted. It was the year of the military draft. We had three months before he left for basic training. From that point on, babies and military transfers came regularly. I was actively involved with my children, my husband, my church, and women's organizations within the military. I loved designing fashions and making them. I enjoyed sewing, teaching, working with children and youth, swimming, singing, drawing, and camping. After fifteen years and two tours in Germany, we left the military and moved to Arizona. I reentered college in 1989 and graduated in 1992, with degrees in Communication and Psychology.

My healing started in Arizona, in 1989, after we got out of the military. Ted's business was failing and he went into a deep depression. In order to handle this, I sought help from a therapist. After seven months, I remember questioning why I was still seeing Tricia. Our sessions had become casual to the point of being art lessons. We would talk about my poetry and drawings for a while and then she would teach me another drawing or painting technique. I learned years later, when I was a therapist, that my drawings and poetry suggested clues that lead her to suspect I had been abused. Although my formal diagnosis was not Multiple Personality Disorder, she began to suspect dissociation. I had no idea of my dissociative coping mechanism.

A totally unexpected phone call on July 18, 1987, at 1:15 in the afternoon, set the wheels of change in motion. My son had turned eleven the day before. I was at a song rehearsal at my friend Laura's house. Our laughter and joyous state were shattered as I listened intently on the phone. My shock must have been apparent as I heard the words that my youngest son had to be taken to the hospital by two o'clock. The doctor would be waiting. I can't reveal the reason for the hospitalization, except to say that it brought up earlier fears I had had for my son. When we arrived at the hospital, we were briefly shown around and then I was told I had to leave. I couldn't stay with my son!

The next thing I recall was finding myself in Tricia's office. It was dark outside. They told me I had been sitting in my rocking chair with my baby-doll for three days. This was the first occurrence of losing time. Tricia had arrived from her vacation a few hours earlier. I was also told about the personalities that had exposed themselves. Ted had taken time off work, and he was there during the session.

Connie and Anna were the first personalities seen by Tricia and Ted. Connie and Anna took most of the physical and sexual abuse as well as the abandonment and fear when my father would leave. That night Tricia also met Elizabeth, my spiritual self, and Tootie, my first alter[1]. All of these personality states were full alters, so they had a variety of emotions as well as experiences. It wasn't until my session the next morning that Tricia started to learn some of the history of my life that had been guarded for over thirty-eight years. It was also the first time Ted and I heard the unbelievable diagnosis of Multiple Personality Disorder and all that it entailed.

Ted and I were mystified by the complexity of dissociation and the years it might take to heal. Tricia explained that the average multiple takes eleven to twelve years in therapy. She also explained that multiplicity is usually developed because of repeated severe abuse starting at a very young age. She said there were specific biological characteristics that made it possible

---

[1]*Alter:* A well-defined personality state with a full range of emotions and functions. Alters will usually create a structure of other personality states for their benefit and use.

to cope in this dissociative manner, some of which might include a high level of hypnotizability, extreme sensitivity to people, environment, and energy, high IQ, exceptional ability to imagine, extreme creativity, and extrasensory perception. Tricia explained that it would be necessary for me to learn about the other personality states and how they functioned in my behalf. All of this information seemed overwhelming and difficult to comprehend.

As my history gradually unfolded, we learned that every human has three parts that come together to create the birth person. These parts are the Spiritual self, the Intellect (historian), and the Emotional. In most people these parts are integrated before birth. In my case these three parts never completely integrated. If I hadn't been abused, they would have eventually integrated on their own, after birth.

Tootie was my first alter. She gained her autonomy when I was about fifteen months old. My mother didn't believe in doctors, so she tried homeopathic remedies to no avail. Garlic enemas, mustard plasters that would leave huge blisters on my chest, and doses of cod liver oil were routinely given. Each of these modalities was traumatizing. There was a time when I had a high fever that would not subside; her methods did not heal me. For my body to heal, I, the birth person, was taken inside and Tootie took my place. This meant that the functioning areas of my brain became isolated and dormant in order to heal. Other areas of my brain developed, took on new internal identities, and functioned in the outside world on my behalf. Tootie was a nickname given to me by my father. I suppose it seemed only appropriate for my first alter to take on that name. Her exuberance for life was unsurpassed. She was the ray of sunshine that shone through even the darkest of clouds.

Tootie functioned in my place for nine years, usually appearing as age three. During the healing years, she became strong and held more energy than any other personality state, including me. If she saw something from the inside, or my birth children mentioned her name, I couldn't hold her back.

Through existing, and new, traumas of anger, abandonment and fear, Tootie eventually created five other personality states. She kept the traumatic memories of my parents arguing and my father's periodic leaving.

After my father's return from Korea, he would leave for days or weeks at a time. I was too young to know where he went. When he was home, my parents would usually argue. My mother always seemed to have the upper hand. I learned early in life that I could never do anything well enough to satisfy her, so my father became my ally. I was his "princess." I knew I was safe with him. He never abused any of his children. Although my father seldom held or cuddled Tootie or me, there seemed to be a naturally deep bond between us; when he was away, it felt as if he took a part of my heart with him.

My father's leavings were always abrupt and unexpected. He would just walk out slamming the door behind him, leaving me behind without a word. He would also return as unpredictably as he left. After an extremely harsh argument, my father left as usual. He returned several days later bandaged from head to toe and hardly able to move. He had fallen asleep in the sun for several hours, but in her childhood innocence, Tootie related her father's condition to the arguing and fighting. If that is what happens when you get mad, Tootie wanted no part of it.

The relationship must have deteriorated badly, because my mother accused my father of seeing other women. One morning, after my father had gone to work, my mother and uncle packed all our belongings in a truck and moved my two brothers and me to a dark, scary apartment building far away. I was upset and afraid that my father would never be able to find us; I didn't know if I would ever see him again.

We hadn't lived in the apartment very long before a strange man started coming around. Mel would bring us presents and was friendly with my mother. Even so, I didn't like him; he was scary to me. By the time I was nine, my mother and Mel had married secretly in Las Vegas. Connie and Anna, two of my alter personality states, became a large part of my life after our move to Wyoming with Mel. Connie took the physical and Anna the sexual abuse from Mel. Other alters and fragments were highly functional during the years my mother and Mel were together. Ruth was one of several personality states that emerged to hold all the anger.

My life became one of secrecy, and daily mental, emotional, physical, and sexual abuse. I knew that when my mother left for her night job, Mel would come to my room and perpetrate rituals that incorporated physical and sexual torture, including rape. At times he would drag my brothers and me out of bed and tie me to a tree in the back yard. He would then force my brothers to watch while he abused me. Mel threatened to kill our mother if the three of us said anything.

One night after Mel and my mother had had a particularly bad argument, Mel showed up in my room. I tried to pretend I was asleep. As he raped me, Anna took over in my behalf. I guess Mel heard one of my brothers coming up the stairs because he put a pillow over Anna's face and held it there until she stopped breathing. My spirit self was watching the events, and as I (Anna), was dying, I remember going through a tunnel toward an incredibly bright light. When I reached the top I was in the most beautiful garden and meadow setting I had ever seen. There were three beings of light waiting for me. They were my Heavenly Father, Heavenly Mother, and Christ. I ran into Christ's outstretched arms. The three personages expressed their love in action and words. Christ held me on his lap until another being of light brought a baby lamb. As I slipped off Christ's lap, the lamb was placed there. I petted the lamb while the three beings of light spoke gently to me.

I was given the choice to stay there or return to complete my mission on earth. I felt their unconditional love in every fiber of my being. I wanted other little girls, like me, to know about this kind of love, so I chose to live. Elizabeth, my spirit self, guided me back into my limp body. After Mel left the room, I put my clothes back on and fell asleep, still knowing and feeling those heavenly arms around me.

The abuse grew worse in every way when we moved to Santa Maria, California, near Vandenburg Air Force Base, where my stepfather had been transferred.

During the four years of healing, Tricia used many modalities: hypnotherapy, sand play, puppets, art, music, dreams, anger release, holding, bonding, and touch therapies. Through automatic writing, and Elizabeth's guidance, we learned a great deal about my tightly closed system. Elizabeth, my spiritual alter, and Sarah, my historian, worked diligently to provide Tricia with the necessary personality states and information for healing.

On April 30, 1990, I, the birth person, was brought back to function in this physical realm. Thirty-eight years had passed, during which time all of my personality states had functioned as me. We stopped counting after two hundred.

One evening, Elizabeth told Tricia that she would be bringing forth a new entity. She was referring to me! Elizabeth came to me inside and beckoned me to follow her. I had spent much time inside with this kind, gentle, and wise being, so I trusted her. She had taught me about the outer world and the people who were to be in my life. With great anticipation, I followed her. Immediately, as if by magic, we were in a place of new intrigue and awareness. It was as though I were looking through a veil at a piece of the world Elizabeth had so eloquently described. Tricia, Ted, and Sheryl (my main host[2]) were standing by the door to leave after a session. I had only dreamt of seeing these three people, and, there they were. They were not aware that Elizabeth and I, "the new entity" (and birth person) were in their presence.

Tricia was holding the most beautiful thing I had ever seen. A crystal heart with a butterfly carved into it. Even more intriguing was the sound of Tricia's voice. She said, "I want you to have this heart, and every time you see it, remember that someday you will soar like a butterfly." Elizabeth gently took my hand in hers and stretched forth my arm. Tricia then placed this beautiful talisman in my hand. I could hardly believe it! I had

[2]*Host*: The alter personality or birth person that is the primary functioning agent at the time.

something of my very own from the blue-eyed angel whom I had grown to love from Elizabeth's teachings.

The next thing I knew, Elizabeth and I were back in the meadow within the recesses of my mind. I was too excited to sleep. Elizabeth explained that I would be leaving this meadow very soon. I would be going to take my rightful place. I was to live in the physical realm with Tricia, Ted, and all the other kind people she had told me about. It was with high anxiety and equal excitement that I received her words and instructions. I fell asleep with the crystal heart clutched tightly in my hand. Tricia's words echoed through my mind. "Someday, you will soar like a butterfly." I could only imagine how that would feel.

Tricia and Ted were unaware of my brief presence. They didn't know it would be the next day in session that I, the birth person, would be permanently brought forward. The time finally arrived for the session of my "rebirth." At the beginning of that session, Elizabeth instructed Tricia to work with Anna, the alter who had received most of the sexual abuse. Anna was to abreact[3] the time she was suffocated while being raped by her stepfather. Anna and the physical body were nine years old at the time of death. Elizabeth explained that the physical body would not actually die during the abreaction. Anna would be taken inside to a facsimile of the meadow and scene that she had previously experienced. Tricia called Anna forward from the recesses of my mind. She was told about the work to be done, but not of the replicated scene inside. Anna started to cry with joy. She wanted to return and stay in that beautiful place of peace and love.

As the abreaction started, Elizabeth came inside to my meadow. She summoned me to follow her. We stood at the very edge of my meadow; a place I had never been before. The scene before my eyes was somehow familiar as I saw three beings in the most beautiful meadow I could ever imagine. The beings were my Heavenly Father, Jesus, and my Heavenly

---

[3]*Abreaction:* One experiences the emotions and details in the released cell memory of a past event as if the event were happening in the present.

Mother. I started to rush into their open arms to feel their loving embrace, when Elizabeth caught my hand. She told me it wasn't time. I was to watch and see what was to happen. Just then, Anna appeared and was embraced by the arms of the three beings. Jesus knelt down in front of Anna. As he talked, Anna listened very intently. Even though I couldn't hear what was being said, I followed Elizabeth as she moved forward into that wondrous place within my mind. Somehow, as I moved into the space Anna occupied, some of her thoughts and feelings of the original event became mine. We were integrated as one being.

The next thing I knew, Elizabeth and I were descending arm-in-arm down a tunnel that was filled with brilliant white light. I felt cheated somehow. I didn't get to stay in that beautiful meadow with those heavenly beings. Had I done something wrong? Why couldn't I stay longer? Was I too bad to stay? What was happening? Where were we going? What was going to happen next?

All these questions raced through my mind during our descent, but were stopped abruptly as I felt myself land against something soft. I was too frightened to open my eyes. Where was this place? What was I feeling? My hands felt the soft fuzzy texture of the chair I was sitting in. The surrounding environment was still and quiet. With my eyes still tightly closed, my hands caressed my face. The awareness of my body sent inquisitive thoughts to my mind. What was this long stringy stuff on the top of my head? My features seemed so different. I could hardly believe that I was feeling my body. My body! I hadn't felt it since I was a child. At that instant everything changed, even new thoughts and awareness, like "I am good! I am a daughter of God! I have an important mission on this earth! The arguing wasn't my fault! I am good! I am good!"

Perhaps it was this realization that prompted me to open my eyes and become completely aware of my new environment. It was just as Elizabeth had promised. Tricia and Ted were there. I think they were as astonished about my presence as I was. They talked softly and seemed to be excited. I could hear

Elizabeth within the chambers of my mind. She kept reassuring me that I was not in any danger and I could trust these people.

At that moment, Elizabeth vanished. I couldn't see or hear her inside. She had told me I would have to experience things on my own for a time, but I didn't know I would be cut off from her completely. What would I do if I got frightened? What if I was in danger and didn't know it? How would I know whom I could trust? Trust. I had done that as a newborn infant. I had trusted my mother and father to care for me and keep me safe from harm. All I recalled was how unsafe I had felt as a baby. As a result of not being taken care of, I, the birth person, was taken inside. Now, thirty-eight years later, I was expected to trust people I hardly even knew. Why would this world be safe now? I realized that I could trust Elizabeth's judgment. I knew she would only leave me with "safe" people, so I put my trust in her. I felt calmer, and determined that I could do this. After all, Elizabeth did say she would only be inaccessible for a short span of time. With the exception of a brief encounter before I left Tricia's office, things remained this way for four days.

Tricia had other clients to see, and Ted had to go to work. They arranged for me to go to Laura's house until Ted got off work. Laura was the closest friend to many of my personality states. She had attended many of our sessions, and had transcribed several tapes of sessions, so she knew me better than I knew myself. Later that day, Ted came and got me. He took me to my "new" external home. I met three of the four children: Michelle, Devin, and Dan. I was eagerly accepted by everyone in my new realm of existence. I learned about my new world by listening, tasting, and touching everything I could. Ted, Tricia, Michelle, Devin, Dan, or Laura were with me at all times to shelter and protect me. On my fifth day in this physical world, a flood of memories and voices resounded in my head. I didn't understand what was happening. Suddenly Elizabeth appeared inside. I could finally see and hear her again within the recesses of my mind.

I didn't understand. Where were the other voices and noises

coming from? I was scared! I didn't know what was happening. Had the past four days been unsafe after all? Was my past coming back to haunt me? Elizabeth calmed my troubled thoughts and explained. Yes, the voices were those from my past, but they were nothing to be afraid of. I was to receive (into my area of the brain), all of the memories, feelings, and experiences of the others.

It took four days to "download" into my memory the information from the past forty years of my life. It was like taking individual disks and downloading them into the hard drive. Everything came in waves, and quickly. Some information was in chronological order: going through the different grades in school, the teachers and friends I had in each grade, traumas, abuse of various kinds, and significant good people entering my life. Other experiences came in groups of events: birthing all four of my children, dating, learning math, and developing various talents. I thought I was being completely silent as the scenes played out before me. I found out later that half of every event was recited out loud (as if a bystander would only hear one side of a telephone conversation).

I gradually became aware and co-conscious[4] with several of my other personality states. Anna and many of her offspring had integrated[5] at the moment I took her place in the meadow within my mind. This was followed by my transformation and rebirth into the physical outer world. Now, since the "downloading," I had everyone's memories. I knew what had happened to them. It was during the time of transferring memories to me, that other personality states automatically integrated. They had finally been able to verbalize and release their trauma.

---

[4] *Co-conscious:* The birth or host personality is able to see and sometimes able to act with the presenting personality state.

[5] *Integration:* A process of bringing all personality states into a final, functioning unit (the birth person). This process is accomplished in stages:
1. Bringing together of all ego states into their creating fragment personality state.
2. Bringing together of the fragmented states into the creating alter.
3. Bringing together of the alters into the first host alter.
4. Bringing the original host alter together with the birth person.
5. The combining of the intellect, spirit, and birth person.

I could hardly believe Tricia had worked with the other personality states within. I had all this knowledge, but didn't know how to run the computer program. It was as though I was living in two worlds at the same time: the outside world, where I was expected to function as an adult with all of the adult responsibilities; and the inside world, where I tried to understand my life from a child's perspective.

There were times when things were overwhelming, when it seemed my family forgot that I was new at experiencing life. Many times I would burst into tears from frustration and overwhelm. My family just couldn't understand, and I couldn't explain. After several weeks of this, Elizabeth consulted with Tricia. I was finally allowed to retreat into the recesses of my mind periodically to watch the others function in my behalf. This meant that I didn't have to be upfront and could allow switching to occur when necessary.

I had to become involved in my own life now. I possessed an undeniable resolve to learn and understand all about my life and about those who had experienced it for me. Sara, my historian and record keeper, also acquired the responsibility of taking care of the internal children. I loved listening to her British accent. Tootie's childlike innocence and spontaneity brought joy from inside. I loved and cherished Tanya's exuberance, Nataly's sensitivity, Pamela's and Deloras's determination, Susan's and Madeline's professionalism, and Stacey's talents. I grew to love and appreciate the two hundred plus parts of me, as well as the people and events in my outside world. I also felt the gnawing burden of it.

Tricia, my therapist, always went the extra mile on my behalf. We attended seminars together and talked personally to presenters who were experts in treating Multiple Personality Disorder. Tricia even arranged to fly us to Des Moines, Iowa, for a private meeting with Chris Costner Sizemore: Eve from *The Three Faces of Eve.*

This experience was incredible! She looked at my mapping[6]

[6]*Mapping*: A graphic illustration of the functioning personality system. This mapping may change periodically. There is usually a mapping for each level of personality states.

of the first level of alters– the only one known at that time–and at all the drawings, and read the poetry my internal selves had written. She gave Tricia and me new understandings and perspectives. Most impressive of all was that she understood "my language." I didn't have to have Elizabeth "interpret," or try to explain things in several different ways to be understood. I now had an ally! Chris told us of her heartaches at finding more personality states. Her therapists had claimed to the whole nation that she was cured. They wouldn't listen to her! She talked about her own struggles of finding a new therapist and having to protect herself from further exploitation. This incredible lady had weathered the storm and come out on the other side. She was integrated and whole! Chris's entire being resonated love, understanding, acceptance, and success. She had been integrated for twelve years at the time. That was the most indescribable day of my life! I had finally met someone like me. I wasn't so freaky after all. I could finally believe that a total integration was not a death of all my selves; it was a new free life for us.

My first major integration took place in the Des Moines hotel that night. Tricia used the imagery of the life stages of the butterfly. As far as we knew, all the parts on the first level chose to integrate at this time. They met together and a chrysalis was formed around us to provide peace, comfort, and love. As our thoughts and energies blended, we became one integrated person. I, as the butterfly, ascended. It felt as though my whole body was filled with incredible white light. The silence was deafening, but I felt great peace and calmness. After returning home from Des Moines, things weren't as overwhelming as they had been. Colors were brighter and things were more dimensional. We thought I was whole and completely integrated. Accessing information became effortless. My two worlds melded almost into one.

Approximately two weeks later, I started hearing a voice in my head again. It sounded like Tootie. Sure enough, as I looked inside, there she was playing on her carousel and having a great time. Elizabeth was sitting in the grass watching her. Where were all the other voices I was hearing? What did this mean? Was this what Chris had described when she discovered more personality states? It was! I tried to keep the knowledge of my discovery to myself. I didn't know how to break the news to Ted or Tricia. My efforts were fruitless. When Tootie saw Tricia, I lost control. I'm not sure who was more disappointed, Ted, Tricia, or I. At that point, I just wanted to quit! Tricia allowed me to make the decision. Unfortunately, I had no peaceful choice in the matter.

Two days later everything broke loose. The whole second level had become exposed. Elizabeth wasn't familiar with the working structure of this level, but she received information from Sarah. This level was mostly composed of fragmented personality states with only a few full alters. Rather than being compartmentalized by individuals, as on the first level, the mapping revealed several fragments located together according to age.

The only exceptions were the jail, Grandpa Aaron, and Aeron. The jail contained the most violent ones. Grandpa Aaron guarded the monster door and sometimes played with the children. Aeron, the controller, guarded the rooms and patrolled the hallway. During the third session, in dealing with this level, Lucy escaped. She was thirteen years old and knowledgeable about this level. She was afraid that Aeron would catch her and throw her into the jail for revealing information. Tricia had Elizabeth take her to the beautiful meadow where she could be safe in her new tree house. Thanks to Lucy, Tricia learned how to work with this level and prepare them for integration. Lucy also gave me hope.

It took about a year for this level to be worked with and integrated. I learned a great deal as I observed from a co-conscious state. There were times when I chose not to be conscious and allowed the fragments or alters to express themselves unencumbered. As with the first level, the final integration was preceded by several small ones. Some were spontaneous and some orchestrated and facilitated by Tricia. There had been well over one hundred personality states on this level. The most difficult task was convincing Tootie to accept another complete integration. She had experienced this previously and was quite disgruntled with the fact that she could not take my place as the birth person. She wanted to have Tricia, Ted, and my family's love and affection all to herself. After a few weeks of allowing her exclusive times with Laura, Tricia, and my family, she consented to the integration.

Things were awkward for me after this integration. I had recurring spells of memory loss. My health deteriorated rapidly, and I had a difficult time staying focused. I would go from one project to another, with no rhyme or reason to the sequence. Sometimes I would forget my own name or simple information. My emotions were continually on a roller coaster ride. I would forget which college classes I was to attend. This was probably because of my obliviousness to time. I wasn't losing time, and if asked, I could recall every event that had occurred, complete with details. It seemed as if my mind was not completely connected to my body. My family tried to be patient as I struggled with short term memory lapses. My instructors at school allowed me to work at my own pace on assignments. They continually encouraged me to keep going. I eventually devised a tracking and reminder system, externally and internally, to train my brain to focus and be more conscious of time.

The situation gradually improved and life became less overwhelming. School was going great until one day, just as I entered my Spanish class with Laura, the sound of a student's voice and the fluency of his speech seemed to pierce my soul. My instructor, Mrs. Accino, and another student were conversing fluently in Spanish. My whole body started to ache. I felt light-headed and emotionally distraught. I was disoriented and unable to focus. Laura drove me to see Tricia. By the time we got there, I could hardly walk. I lay on the couch in the large office room while Tricia finished with her client.

Visual flashbacks and body memories revealed that I had been kidnapped from my apartment by two Mexicans when I was nineteen. I had seen the two men around the area before, so I was not startled when they first approached me. They were

Carol

137

conversing in Spanish so I couldn't understand them. They seemed agitated. The tallest one grabbed me and forced me into their car. They tied my hands with a belt. The driver and the man in the back seat with me kept talking and yelling at me. He started hitting me and blocked any attempt I made to keep him away. It seemed as if minutes had turned to hours until the man next to me got out of the car. I was weak and bleeding from being hit in the face. The driver took me up to a place on the side of a hill. After raping, beating, and threatening me, then cutting my leg with his knife, he left abruptly. I could see a familiar, brilliant white light in the distance coming down from the heavens.

It was during the abreaction that I recalled the most incredible events of the kidnapping. I had the intervention of a higher power. I remembered the flash of red from a vehicle that must have panicked my abductor, who had left me for dead. The next things I recalled were reentering my battered body, and the pain of being lifted from the ground into the car. I remembered becoming conscious off and on and seeing the kind, loving faces of an older man and lady by my bedside. They were surrounded by extraordinary light that seemed to come from the center of the ceiling and filter down to fill the whole room. I was torn between wanting to ascend to the apex of the light, and wanting to stay in the unbelievable environment in which my body dwelt. I finally chose to live. The next few days I was cared for and nurtured back to health by Edith and Oliver. I had never known more loving and gifted people. A few days later, they drove me back to my apartment. I made mental notes of my surroundings so that I could return with a gift of thanks for my caretakers. A few days later when I was stronger, I drove back to the exact spot of their home. I found a vacant lot. According to the city records, there had never been a house there.

By the time Tricia arrived at my side, I was hardly breathing. Laura had been monitoring my vital signs as my condition grew worse. It was the memory of that divine intervention, and my previous decision to live, that started turning my situation around. Later that day, it was apparent that another level had emerged. Tootie and Elizabeth were once again separate.

As if that wasn't enough, Tootie returned depressed. She announced her desire to go to heaven to be with her daddy. My earthly father had died prior to my healing from the kidnapping, and Tootie knew where he was. Even though she was told she would have to leave Elizabeth, Ted, Laura, and her new family that she had grown to love, her mind was made up. Elizabeth advised Tricia to give Tootie permission, on the condition that Tootie would give all her memories, emotions, and thought patterns to her twin, Trudy. She agreed, and was left simply with the memory of the love she held for her father. Little did Tootie know that Elizabeth would take her only to the beautiful meadow inside, the same meadow where Anna had appeared with the heavenly beings when she integrated with me. A final integration could not take place while Tootie was there. In light of all that had happened, we decided that rather than traumatize Tootie any further, her request would be granted. The exchange was made. Trudy had become like Tootie, except that she was calmer and easier to deal with.

By this time, I wasn't sure integration was worth all the effort and disappointment. It took a few days to recover physically and emotionally from all that had transpired. Trudy was out front quite a bit during my recovery time. It was fun to see her interact with my family, Laura, and Tricia. Other than school, the performing group, and church, our relationship circle was quite limited.

Trudy was more accepting of the healing process than Tootie had been. This made working with, and integrating the third level relatively smooth. I noticed more shifting of my abilities and recall after that integration. Trudy was the only one holding the third level integration and connection with me at the time.

Another new personality state handled the Spanish class. Her name was Caren Marie. By this time in the school year, my Spanish instructor had gained a little understanding of multiplicity through hearing my lectures at the college and interacting with us during class.

After graduating, I was offered a permanent job in the clinic owned and operated by Tricia and her husband Kendell. I was able to work with my own clients, under Kendell's license. I was also able to get my hypnotherapy certification. Everything was going extremely well. It seemed I was fully integrated, except for Trudy and Elizabeth. Trudy had many restraining limits enforced by Elizabeth, so there would not be any interference while working with clients. I was content with this level of integration.

Tricia, Kendell, and I attended a three-day seminar on Multiple Personality Disorder. By the end of the third day we were exhausted. That night in the hotel suite, they watched the movie *Fried Green Tomatoes*. I sat in the other room drawing. I remember hearing a scene involving a child getting run over by a train. I realized I had seen the film before, so I went on drawing. The next day, as we were driving home, we heard the whistle from a train in the distance. I only caught a glimpse of the train before the consciousness of my exterior world vanished. I had been overtaken by a terror-stricken child (fragment[7]), in the middle of an abreaction. By the time we arrived home, several fragments and ego states[8] from this one incident, had made their appearance. Each personality state abreacted their role. Ellen, the main personality, depicted the most traumatizing and horrifying event we had discovered. She couldn't speak, only react.

The event centered on my rape by Draper, my stepfather's father. I was only eight years old. He tied my arms and legs, spread-eagle, to posts in the barn. He said it was because of me that the hobo was hit by the train and killed. Draper said bad girls needed to be punished. I felt helpless! That was the first time I had been raped and threatened. I felt as if I was being ripped open and set on fire inside. He urinated in my mouth as he held my cheeks tight and my mouth open. I thought I was

[7] *Fragment*: A personality state, less defined, that only holds one emotion for several events, or several emotions for one event. An evolved ego state. A fragment may be connected to several ego states.

[8] *Ego State*: A personality state carrying one event and one emotion, or a portion of an event with one emotion.

going to die! He threatened me with a pitchfork as he shoved it toward my face, between my legs, and around my body. Mei (meaning me, myself, and I), my alter and protector created at that time, along with twenty-five others, never revealed how we survived and got away.

Two more levels and over thirty-five personality states were now exposed. After working for several hours, I was finally able to return to the foreground. I had seen and heard everything! I was in a state of shock and severe depression. In a matter of seconds, the life I had worked so long and hard for, had vanished. Everything seemed so hopeless!

Suicide attempts became a daily event. I was put on a round-the-clock watch; my family, Tricia, and Laura all took part. Tricia and Kendell talked about hospitalizing me. Tricia was afraid, however, that being in a strange environment with new people, would be even more traumatizing. Elizabeth had petitioned more spiritual healers, helpers, and protectors. That's when Mirium arrived. Some kind of barrier was put in place to separate the self-destructive ones. When I was inside, I was held and sung to by Mirium and the others. Mei was the protector of two levels of injured personalities. There were many who could not even speak or converse clearly. The self-destructive personalities were now under the watchful eye of a guardian angel. When Elizabeth or I were not forward, Mei was. Because of my depression, I wasn't out very much. Elizabeth discovered a journal entry that depicted several of the ego states conversing with each other. Tricia finally had the connection she needed to work with the third level, and understand the fourth.

I gradually became more hopeful and started functioning in my life again. I saw the effects of this period on my family, and was concerned. They were weary of the turmoil. My children wanted their real mother back. My daughter, Michelle, escaped by going to college in Hawaii. My oldest son, Fred, moved out on his own to an apartment. Devin spent most of his time with his friends, and Dan seemed to withdraw into his own little world. My husband became unsure that any integration would stay complete. The only personality who could bring a sense of joy to our home was Trudy. I prayed and prayed for all the turmoil to end. My body and mind were exhausted. I know Tricia was exhausted also.

It took about six months to work with and integrate these two levels. It was also on these two levels that the greatest amount of anger emerged with unexpected force. Tricia, Kendall, Ted, Dan (my son), and I were spending a few days together in a mountain cabin. It was during a session at the cabin that the depth of my anger was unleashed with such brute strength that it took all three men to hold me down so I would not harm myself or anyone else. Tricia had often reminded me that as long as I held onto bitterness, resentments, anger and destructive emotions, I would not be free. She said I was still allowing my perpetrators to abuse me. Those words just added fuel to the fire that was burning deep inside. By the time this session was over, we were all completely exhausted. I had never felt so tired and so free!

I had often worked on forgiveness issues during various therapy sessions, but never before had I faced the total engulfment of its force from the years of abuse. The release of the anger and the newfound freedom allowed me to reach the pinnacle of forgiveness. I started by forgiving myself for not acknowledging my own innate worth as a daughter of God. I also asked my inner selves for forgiveness for anything I might have done to magnify their pain, and acknowledged each part for all s/he had done for me. I had a great support team to teach me how to love myself. The more I loved myself, the more I was able to forgive others. My greatest challenge was to forgive and honor my physical body. It had been the object of the abuse. The cellular memory was a powerful, graphic, and painful reminder of all that had happened. Several hours of Rapid Eye, massage, craniosacral, Reiki, DNA release, therapeutic touch, and sensory stimulation were instrumental in this difficult forgiveness process.

It was also during this time that Tricia's cancer, which had been in remission, reemerged. She stopped seeing all but one other multiple and me. I discontinued seeing any clients, and became Tricia's caretaker. I was afraid of losing her. Eventually, I returned to work at the clinic.

As both Tricia and I grew stronger each day, I felt unsettled about her decision to move to Young, Arizona, despite the fact that Young was only three hours away. My husband, Ted, and I had moved a small trailer next to their home on their old property. Being busy at the clinic, I seldom spent time with Laura. I also withdrew from Tricia—seeing boxes being packed and the move being carried out, was too painful

Kendell wanted me to take over the center. I declined. Sharon, a Rapid Eye Technician, and Don, another psychologist, accepted Kendell's offer. One condition of the sale was that I would always have a place to practice in the clinic. The terms were agreed upon and the transaction was final. Kendell and Tricia moved to Young. Trudy had lost her mommy, and I had lost my closest friend and confidant.

About a week later, a friend and I walked in on an armed robber in my house. I was so panicked, I froze. This is just how I had responded to similar situations as a child and teenager. My friend pulled me outside and called the police. I was too anxious to go back inside my house.

That evening I had an appointment to counsel a ritually abused client; she was in crisis. I had already prepared my client to meet Sharon in order to experience Rapid Eye Therapy. I had heard that by using this healing modality, a client didn't need to abreact the trauma to heal. In this situation, however, Sharon was not experienced in working with Satanic Ritual Abuse, so that as my client worked with Sharon, she abreacted a Grand Sacrifice Ritual. I was used to seeing scenes played out in my clients' minds. Tricia said it was a rare gift. At that moment especially, it seemed like a curse. Unfortunately, I was experiencing the full ceremony, as if in proxy for my client. I could feel the sword in my hand, my heart about to burst from my chest, and the intense pain of slaughtering the baby. The taste of bloody flesh in my mouth and the stench of body parts being burned in the flames of purification, was almost too much to handle. I was finally able to call Elizabeth forward, as I re-treated inside to Mirium's arms.

It was not unusual for me to connect with my ritual abuse (RA) clients because of the familiarity of the patterned events. When my stepfather abused me, I learned to know how bad the abuse would be depending on how long and extensively my parents argued. After my mother would leave for work, Mel would sit down and play the organ loudly. The tones were intensely penetrating and frightening to me as he played one dissonant chord after another, with no rhyme or reason. It would remind me of something you might hear in a haunted house or horror movie. It certainly meant horror for me! Although there was no cult abuse, this was only one of many rituals.

Later that night, after the robbery and dealing with the RA client, I had my first Rapid Eye session. Two of the personality states that had been previously integrated had reappeared. They were the child and teen who had been created during previous robberies. (When I was about six, I entered the house after play-ing outside and discovered a man armed with a wrench. My brother, who was about seven, then burst into the house. My memory is somewhat hazy, but I believe the sight of not one, but two children, frightened the man. He left. Again, when I was a teenager, I was awakened from sleep by becoming aware of a light in the darkened house. I got up and found a man in the midst of a robbery. By the time I alerted my parents, the robber was gone.) After my second session, I was able to return home without any problem, and both personality states were spontaneously reintegrated.

About one month after the robbery, my family had moved into Tricia's home until it sold. I walked in on a robbery again. This time I chased the guy! I realized I had gotten to the core of that issue and wondered what else had not been cleared com-pletely.

I turned my clients over to other therapists the night of the first robbery. I wanted to take a break before seeing clients again. I was feeling overwhelmed. Within four weeks, Tricia had moved, we had the robbery, I witnessed by proxy a Satanic ritual, experienced a cruel defamation of character by Don, and lost my office. I was devastated! It took me about a year to put these experiences behind me.

Ten months later, I took Rapid Eye Training. It changed my life! The training was definitely a transforming experience. Tootie returned from the meadow in the recesses of my mind. Trudy automatically integrated with Tootie at that time, and Tootie claimed her rightful place.

Four months after that, Ted and I moved to Utah. I had been offered a partnership in the healing center. We were in Utah ten days when all the business partners were called to the Rapid Eye Institute in Oregon. While there, Ranae, the director, learned that I had never experienced re-birthing. She insisted it be completed before we left Oregon. The session was arranged for that evening. Tootie chose two of the trainers she had grown to trust. She wanted to be the one to do the session, so Tootie started and I finished. By the end of that incredible experience, I realized that Tootie and Elizabeth were completely integrated. I couldn't even see their meadow, the carousel, the castle, or anything else that had become so familiar and safe. Mirium was also gone. Everything was deafeningly quiet. I was exhausted. Pam, Ranae, and the trainers were all congratulating me. All I could feel was the isolation!

Instead of going to training the next day, Pam and Donna, two of my business partners, took me to Portland. I slept during most of the drive. On the way, we came across the "Largest Sitca Tree in the United States." As I stood on the platform that encircled the base of the tree, I looked up. It was like seeing my whole life graphically portrayed within the life of that majestic tree. It was so tall, the top seemed to disappear into the heavens. Cascading down the enormous trunk was a massive scar. It started far above my view, weaving through the branches and ending well below them. The branches, extending in a maze at the top of the tree, seemed to depict the intricate, yet complex alter system of my past. The scar represented the traumatic events of my life. As I focused on the huge trunk, I noticed the reciprocal action of life and nurturing between the tree and the many species of plants and animals. I climbed under the surrounding platform to observe the grand root system that nurtured the tree. I stood between two roots. They wrapped around and embraced me in their life-giving force. I felt loved and safe.

My partners created a congratulatory integration ceremony. They stood at the base of the tree, on the platform. I walked up the ramp to the beat of their drums until I stood in front of them. The rain fell in a light mist, like cleansing dew. Touching me with a fallen Sitca branch, on one shoulder and then the other, they gave me a new name: "Healing Sitca." It was an unforgettable experience that brought closure to my past and hope for a new future. The next two days of training were enlightening. Before we left, Ranae presented me with her personal crystal turtle. She said the turtle represented me well; it was a totem of honor and leadership. At that moment, I felt as majestic as the trees.

Life was not perfect after that. At times I felt very lonely. Accessing the talents and abilities of the alters was different from before. I had to learn all over again. Our new business was demanding and time consuming. Many important decisions had to be made. We lost a business partner and moved our location to Orem, Utah. My preconceived ideas about "life after integration/fusion" were far from accurate. My health declined again. My vision went through many changes, far different from before. Sometimes the pain in my body was so severe that I tried, without success, to separate again. Waves of despair and suicidal ideation would be replaced temporarily by fear and paranoia. I was on a roller coaster of uncontrolled emotions. As I released these emotions, my life gradually equalized. Ted and I cut back on our work days and had more personal time.

My granddaughter, Sierra, and her parents, Fred and Jenny, moved into the basement of Ted's and my home. Sierra became a light in my life, and a major reason for living. Although it was difficult, Ted and I were learning to share our emotions. He still didn't trust my integration/fusion to be solid and complete. As

I waited through the months for proof, I continued to learn more about myself and our relationship. Ted and I were strengthening our relationship as husband and wife. The most difficult things to learn were social and personal people skills. To assist me with these challenges, I participated in a Personal Empowerment Seminar and a Relationship Seminar. Each training presented major challenges that had a profound impact on my life.

In the Relationship Seminar, I had the opportunity to improve my relationship with my daughter and husband. I still had difficulty defining my role as a mother versus a therapist. One day my daughter came to me when she was dealing with some difficult issues. I asked if I could help her through them. She said she needed me to be her Mom, not her therapist. That concerned me; I knew how to help her as a therapist, but the only thing I knew how to do as a Mom was to give her love and a listening ear. Somehow that seemed inadequate. As I prayed, I was given confirmation that unconditional love was the greatest gift I could give as a mother. I was relieved and grateful.

Approximately eighteen months after my integration, another change took place within me. As I prayed for answers, I was directed to go through the process I call fusion/absolution[9]. Rather than *functioning* as one whole being, we would *be* one whole being, which included body, mind, and spirit. The next day, I drove up to my favorite place in the canyon. Sitting by the edge of the rushing stream, I watched the beautiful autumn leaves fall gracefully to the ground and lie at the base of the changing trees. As I pondered my situation and the life cycle of the tree before me, I gained a new understanding about fusion/

[9] *Fusion/Absolution:* The process of connecting the body, mind, and spirit to this physical dimension. This is the final process, which is also completed in stages.
1. Release all cellular memories.
2. Become completely connected to your body in this physical dimension.
3. Know for certainty that your integration is complete. (To always be at choice and able to act, instead of react, from connections to the past.)
4. Feel your innate worth and strengths. (At this point a completely new coping mechanism has been adapted and is functional in a healthy manner. There can no longer be separation. I know. I've tried!)

absolution. The leaves that had fallen and now surrounded the trunk of the tree represented my personality states. The trunk and branches of the tree represented my body and mind. The leaves would turn into mulch. The mulch would transform into nutrients that would course through the veins of the tree, providing structure for new life to begin. I realized that no part would be lost. They would provide the structure and connection so that I could start a new life. Nothing would be solid. Everything would be fluid, like the water in the stream. I could obtain a complete balance of body, mind, and spirit. This new understanding brought more hope and meaning to my soul.

I have met many challenges during this year since fusion/absolution. I was physically near the gates of death. My Heavenly Father told me that I could choose to return to him or continue to live. Either decision would be acceptable. There were two conditions to living: live my life in joy; only consider my own feelings. I was not to live because of, or for, someone else. I wanted to find out what that would be like, so I chose to live. Shortly after I made this decision, my physical body started responding to medical treatment. I am now on my quest of finding joy in every day of my life.

I have never been more at peace within, nor had as strong a desire to live. My ability to love my husband, family, and others has never been so unencumbered. My mother is now my friend. She divorced Mel after he became excessively abusive to her. I have forgiven my perpetrators, including Mel, for what they did to me. Most of all, I have forgiven myself! I know the multiplicity was a gift for my survival and life mission, and so was my healing.

It is with much gratitude to Judy Dragon and Terry Popp, that I include part of my story. This writing has been cathartic and revealing. I can now see how far I have come, and the strength I have to Claim My Light! I have also been able to reflect with gratitude on those caring individuals who assisted me in my healing. I have many "Earthly Angels" in my life. I know there will be difficult times ahead, but if I can overcome this, I can do anything! I look forward to the learning.

Terry

*I am a writer, editor, teacher, living in a state of continuing grace that
happens to coincide, at this time, with the San Francisco Bay Area. Having
found my own voice through telling my story in written form, I enjoy helping
others give voice to their stories.*

Breath is life. One talks about God who breathed life into his
creations; about the Muses who breathe inspiration into
seers, poets, artists. And yet, breathing has always come hard
to me. I entered this world without breath; it took mighty efforts from the delivery staff to induce me to breathe. Why would
I want to breathe? My father had talked my mother into having
three abortions before me. When I was in the womb, I felt her
attempts to eliminate me. How could I know that the outer world
would be any safer than the cradle in which I had rested for
nine months?

FEBRUARY 1987.

*A grain of sand. That's how the baby started. Layer upon layer of
matter, experiences, dreams, memories coat the grain, form the pearl.
Mother of Pearl tried to abort the developing gem, gave birth, then
abandoned the child at three years of age.*

*Who is this child, this me? This child born in Hollywood from the
loins of a mother who didn't, wouldn't take care of her. Mother's milk
of kindness and love, that's what babies deserve, not layers of pain.*

My father left the family in 1929 when I was a year old. Two years later my mother, perhaps in despair, attempted to smother me with a pillow. While the body was deep in shock and struggling to stay alive, what had been my core ruptured and Pearl became my first alter.

After Pearl, fifteen more alters formed to handle the pain and confusion from subsequent traumas.

AUGUST 1987

Memory of splitting. My whole body hurts, aches. A part of me has been ripped away. There is a wrenching ... a bursting out. The splitting leaves the physical pain of the pulling apart and the violent agony of a raw vacuum. Then a thunderous clap, like when a plane breaks the sound barrier and molecules slam back to fill the void.

OCTOBER 1987

Memory of splitting. I look at my hands. They aren't mine. I'm not here. I don't exist. I scream. No colors ... no senses at all ... just pure feeling beyond any kind of terror. I shatter, explode into a thousand pieces. I have no core ... the cooperation of two or more alters are necessary to form a core. Maia [my therapist] says all the pieces will fall back to the ground. That's how I see it ... they'll rain down. Then I'll feel a universe ... a power ... larger ... holding me ... protecting me.

My mother left me at the Infant Shelter in San Francisco when I was between three and four. I'm not certain how long I was there—probably about a year. After that, I lived with different families, including a girlfriend of my father's who involved me in a Satanic Ritual Abuse cult. During those years (from four/five to eight) I was frequently sick—whooping cough, chicken pox, scarlet fever and, finally, a systemic strep infection that almost killed me. When I complained, as I often did, that my legs and hips hurt, I was told to be quiet, that what I was feeling were growing pains. I have good reason to believe that both the illnesses and the pain were a result of cult abuse and experimentation.

When the cult forced me to do what no human being, much less a child, should be asked to do, Mimi split off, shortly joined by Ruth and Miriam, Jr. Some of my alters came in pairs, one embodying the dark, the other the light. Ruth took on the shame and degradation. Miriam, Jr. was tough and sarcastic. She let Ruth know that the killing and mutilation of animals and children were just games and that they both should feel proud of the honors being bestowed upon them: special attention on birthdays, like allowing us to decide who would be tortured, and who spared; the marriage to Satan at age six. Mimi, as a rule, hovered about ten feet off the ground. She watched what was going on but kept her innocence, creating a fantasy world with lovely music, sweet smells, and gems that flashed brilliant colors from the sun she created.

My father wove in and out of my life. During his first sexual molestation of me when I was five, Dolly split off to deal with his betrayal and my shame. When I was eight and went to live with my father and stepmother in San Francisco, the cult abuse stopped. I thought I had finally found a happy, secure home. In my acute disappointment that this was not the case, that my father's marriage only led to more sexual and emotional abuse, I slashed my wrists with a razor blade. Naomi then stepped in and became mother, ruler, taskmistress of the children, vowing that never again would we get close enough to another person for them to hurt us so badly. And never, never would we tell our secrets to anyone. This strategy worked effectively when I was young. However, the negative energy kept me isolated and distanced from people even when, as an adult, I wanted to become intimate.

JANUARY 1988

Darkness surrounds me. Darkness from night activities ... blood sacrifices ... crucifixions ... buried in a coffin with snakes ... forced to watch a little boy's penis cut off while a man plays with my genitals, his genitals ... mind bending, mind numbing rituals ... Satanic cult activities that nearly kill me.

Darkness from Daddy who reads to me Alice in Wonderland,

Through the Looking Glass, A Child's Garden of Verses. *While he reads these lovely, delicate, enchanting words, Daddy plays with my hair, with my soft child's skin, with my barely budded genitals. I hear the sound of the words, their music. That is all.*

My parents sent me to boarding school when I was nine. Two years later we moved to Los Angeles, where I again slashed my wrists, this time with broken glass from a bed lamp smashed by Sylvia—one of three alters who handled adjustments necessary for major moves—after a fight with my father. She was in a suicidal rage after he badly beat us up. Although moving may not seem traumatic to some, for me the moves were often difficult because they entailed being uprooted, locating in a new part of the country, getting acquainted with new people. They sometimes involved coming into contact with people who either had once been in the cult, or who were still involved with the cult.

We lived in Los Angeles for a year before moving to Mexico City. Leo, a family friend who had sexually molested me in San Francisco, then in Los Angeles, turned up in Mexico City for a few days, long enough to molest me again. My parents ignored my pleas not to be left alone with him. Leo's molestation of me resulted in pregnancy. I was then twelve and had started menstruating two years earlier. An abortion was performed by a friend of my parents, a wealthy doctor I believe was involved with the cult.

We lived in Mexico for six months, then moved to New York City. When I was thirteen, my parents sent me to live with a family in a small town north of New York City. While there, I changed my name from Marylou to Terry. Marylou was my mother's name. I hated it. I have no idea why I chose a male name, or why I chose that name. There was a comic strip popular at the time, *Terry and the Pirates.* Perhaps I thought the pirates would protect me. Terry, my one male alter, emerged then. I'm not certain which came first, the alter or the name change, but Terry was certainly my protector. He tried hard to keep me from being harmed by my thirteen-year-old emerging, destructive sexuality. I frequently put myself into dangerous sexual situations—like picking up servicemen at roller skating rinks. Terry once lent wings to my feet when two men cornered my girlfriend, also thirteen, and me. She was raped. When I managed to scramble away from him, the man I was with chased me, waving a broken, jagged beer bottle.

Two years later, my parents decided they wanted me again, and so I went to live with them in Cincinnati. During that year, when I was fifteen, my father called me a slut, a whore, accused me of trying to seduce every man we passed on the street, and then raped me for the last time.

By the time I got to the University of Chicago at sixteen, I had no idea who I was or what my scattered, patchy life was about. Another of my alter pairings came into existence: Golden Girl, who thought life was one big party, and Tess, who lived on drugs and sordid sexual affairs. I shifted back and forth between these two, with my child alters emerging when an event triggered them, like the rape that occurred at a fraternity dance when I was drunk. I flunked out in three years. I had a difficult time studying. I know now that I'm dyslexic. This, plus my difficulty in understanding and retaining information, made test taking problematic. Increasingly, I would simply blank out. The main problem, however, most likely lies in the fact that I have no memory of ever being in a classroom. I can only imagine that the alter who was in all those classrooms was so cut off that most of the information never filtered through.

My years of therapy started while I was in college. I was sent to a psychiatric intern at Student Health. My advisors couldn't figure out why, with my intelligence, I wasn't getting better grades. Now the reason seems obvious. I was on speed, alcohol, three packs of cigarettes a day, coffee and tea from morning till late at night. I got little sleep because my nightmares were so bad I was afraid to go to bed. I didn't see the intern for long. I was terrified of therapists, tense and guarded, not knowing what was safe to divulge. When I was seventeen, a family friend, somehow realizing how badly I needed help, set up an appointment with a psychiatrist for me. The night before the appointment, I took a whole bottle of phenobarbital, never expecting to wake up. When I did, I was in despair. I went to see the psychiatrist once and refused to go back. He had a fatherly air about him; that was probably one of the many things that distressed me.

Tanya and Sonya, another pair, had been with me the entire time, aging as I aged, absorbing the experiences, but not involved with them. While in therapy in 1987, I felt them up in the stratosphere, far away. When they finally landed in my world, it was with a bang and a barrage of anger at my having called them down from their lofty aerie. Sonya raged on and on about how it wasn't their function to feel the horror and pain; they were there merely to record the events. She had a nasty tongue that finally got on Tanya's nerves. They had a showdown and, as a result, Sonya merged into Tanya. In this way, the rage was tempered with compassion.

Alters kept forming until I was in my fifties. The *me* who acted as host was composed of two or more alters, the combination shifting, depending upon the circumstances.

What was it like to have sixteen separate personalities, and numerous fragments, in my one body? Secretive. There were many dark spaces that robbed me of depth; I was two-dimensional. I always felt like an outsider, an observer. I was extremely guarded because I was always afraid I might say the wrong thing, even though I had no idea what the "wrong thing" might be. My life was full of secrets: the fact that my parents were communists; the fact that Lily was not my real mother; the fact that I had a wonderfully creative mind; the fact that I was a multiple. Add to these the fact that the cult told me that my parents, and any one close to me, stood a good chance of dying if I said anything about my cult life, and I had an overflow of unacceptable things about which I could not talk. My whole life seemed cast in darkness. Even on the brightest day my soul was captured, like a caterpillar, in a dark cocoon, and I was kept in the larval stage of imprisoned childhood. All of this felt normal. It was me.

Barbed wire. I am stuck to barbed wire. Hate ... regret ... shame ... sorrow ... rage ... guilt. Red flags ... mangled ... mutilated ... ragged shreds of former lives. Blood from my tortured soul drips away my life force, drop by heavy, hot, sluggish drop.

Turn my torn body away from this red ... livid ... black nightmare of commitment to old ways of seeing, viewing, feeling, not feeling ... from horrors past, lived through, then lived again. How long? How long?

As I mentioned, some of my alters came in pairs. Except for these few pairings, none of my alters knew about the others. That's what made for the secrecy. I heard voices in my head, whispering, talking about things I didn't understand, in a language that meant nothing to me. I never thought to wonder—that is, until 1991—why I never remembered being in a classroom, why I had total amnesia of the time from birth to age eight, and then of additional years, months, days, hours.

I became aware of my extreme overreaction to losing things when, about seven years ago, my lover and I took a car trip up to Oregon. One night, Tao started looking around for his misplaced car keys. I was immediately struck by his calm manner. He looked very methodically and slowly until he found them. I realized in a flash how different his way was from mine. For him, finding those keys was a simple matter. For me, it would have felt like life and death. Sometimes I just lost things, like everybody else, and it was no problem. When I got that *special* feeling in my body, however, I knew an alter had hidden the object and that I probably would never find it. The object could be keys, my glasses, a book, money, time, my sanity, my life.

Keeping my secrets from others was not as difficult as it might have been. Being introverted, inner oriented, reclusive, made it easier. I had no intimate relationships during my childhood and few during my teens. I never lived anywhere long enough to develop friendships. When I went to college at sixteen, I got into drugs and sex. I twice married alcoholics. Hard to have an intimate relationship under those conditions.

JUNE 1991
Over the darkness spreads a layer of light ... sharp, diamond-cutting, crystalline light. The darkness of relationships and marriages carried within them the seeds of wonder, light, delight. Carl ... New York: bright, sharp-tongued ... glowing with ideas ... driven by an intellectual engine that never quit. A poet with moods so dark that at nineteen he had great black circles under his brown eyes. Lenny ... California: a bright shadow, with a black hole. To put a toe in was to court being sucked under. And yet and yet. Playful ... teasing ... full of fun ... eyes maniacally bright under their cool blue exterior. This little girl ... now woman ... me ... in between ... drawn to both ... not knowing my own bleak, black bottoms. A perpetual smile aching my face. Shy/bold. Sweet/sour. Who knew this girl/woman?

Most people who were close to me, like my two husbands, never guessed the truth. What words would they have used? They thought I was neurotic, moody, changeable, an alcoholic. My efficient alter, Margery, held it together during my years of employment, although the strain took a terrible toll. Going to work was a misery: I would feel the clutch of fear in my stomach. Sometimes it was so strong I was afraid I would vomit or faint. I lived in a constant state of tension and apprehension. I thought I would be asked questions I couldn't answer, be called upon to do things that, although I had done them the day or week before, I wouldn't remember how to do, would answer the phone and forget where I was or who I was. I was never really clear about the basis of my fear, I just knew it was there. This fear kept me in inferior positions; anything more challenging than clerical or secretarial work would send me over the edge.

Therapists couldn't figure me out; I grew quite skilled at manipulating them. I knew I needed help badly, but until 1985, the therapists I saw were Freudian analysts who did me more harm than good. The last thing I needed was to be told my fantasies about incest were the wish fulfillments of a childhood Oedipus complex, when, in fact, my father molested me for a number of years. During those years of Freudian therapy, analysts tried to make me believe that the events I was attempting to tell them were symbolic, not real happenings. In other words, when I told them about suspicious encounters with my father, and about situations that seemed to blend torture with sexual feelings, they told me these were symbolic of deeply repressed dreams and wishes.

I kept trying to find someone who would be my ally, someone who could see into me and discover my truth. The fact that I slogged through almost forty years of therapy, off and on, proves how desperately I wanted the darkness to lift, wanted a life better than what I had. The main ingredient of my quest was to find that better life. Almost as important, was my terror of losing my sanity, or succeeding in one of my many suicide attempts. I finally found the right person, Maia, in 1985 and the incest, the ritual abuse and my multiplicity came spilling out.

My life finally made sense—my dreams, my fears, my despair, my physical oddities, had a context. As an adult I had twice been told I was pregnant (in both cases the rabbit died) and was later found not to be pregnant. Kaiser/Permanente ran tests on me for three months and diagnosed me diabetic, prescribed a restrictive diet and gave me pills to take. When I began to faint, a friend suggested I see his doctor. I did. The doctor said I definitely did not have diabetes. I had been diagnosed one day with numerous allergies, a week later with none. My optometrist called me a few years back when I was having new glasses fitted; they couldn't seem to get the prescription right. She said, "I don't understand, each time I test you it comes out differently." By this time I knew what was happening and laughed. She asked me what was funny. All I could say was, "I don't think you'd understand."

I started therapy with Maia because I had been involved in a near fatal automobile accident–the last of three. I had totaled my car and wound up having shoulder surgery. My shoulder healed, but my psyche didn't. I was terrified to drive. I didn't want to go back into therapy, but I knew I'd never drive, or probably survive, if I didn't.

The job of becoming aware of this huge, unwieldy, amnesiac system, and slowly dismantling it, took years of therapy. I became aware of the multiplicity after wondering if perhaps I had a poltergeist, or, worse, the spirit of my dead father, turning on lights in my garage at night, leaving my back garage door wide open when I left the house. From the garage one could easily get into my house. The first time it happened I called the police who came and investigated. They found nothing, no footprints, fingerprints. Nothing. One day Maia looked directly into my eyes. "Do you really not know who that is?" I was stunned by her question. And then it hit me. It was me! I was devastated, sick to my stomach with shame and terror. My secret had been found out. By Maia. And by me.

Many multiples are asked to map their alter system. My alters didn't allow that until the integration was well under way. They were also shy for a long time about revealing their names and talking about their functions. At different times, each one told me I could use any name I wanted, but that I should understand the name was not her/his name.

My therapist and I–the host–had to work hard to build trust. Trust, for me, consisted of being believed. Never in my life had I been believed–not by my parents, my teachers, my peers, my lovers, my therapists. In addition, somewhere in my unconscious was the need to know that the person with whom I worked would be strong enough to stay centered, and feel compassion for me when the horrors that lay locked within my alters were freed and came roaring out. Perhaps even more imperative than the above conditions, was my need to know that the person had a spirituality that could hold both the profane and the sacred that made up my background. I could not have given words to this last condition, but somewhere in my system was an awareness that it was essential.

During the years of recovering painful memories, I wasn't certain whether or not I would make it, or whether I wanted to make it. In addition to therapy, 12-Step meetings became part of my life. I wrote voluminously and kept track of my dreams and therapy sessions. I attempted to meditate, but the timing wasn't right; each time I closed my eyes to concentrate on my breath, or follow a taped meditation, I was flooded with memories, fears and tears. I was as kind as I could be to my body: I swam, walked, had massages, sacro-cranial work, Feldenkrais, acupuncture. Memory work is hard labor.

NOVEMBER 1993

Nightmare. The air around my bed thickens. Compresses. Coagulates. Melts. Undulating, pulsating waves of black, gray fill the room. An alien energy disturbs the air particles, approaches. Men. I feel them. Standing at the foot of my bed. This is not a dream. The men are real. The smell, the dank feel of corruption, of dark, filmy, slimy places. Beings who pierce the matter of my world, penetrate the web I have woven to keep me safe. Their hands reach out, grab my feet. I scream.

My back comes straight off the bed, propelled by the pounding of my trapped heart. My eyes stare. Sweat trickles down my face. My palms are sticky. Oh God. They still come for me, these phantoms from my cult past. These worshippers of Satan. These demons with robes, hoods, chants, who were real then, should be dead now.

I close my eyes again. I will sleep to return. My body floats. My eyes are wide open under their lids, staring. My brain is awake and motionless. No thoughts. No feelings. The flutter of fear starts in the belly. Mimi grabs her teddy bear. The fear ebbs. I open my eyes. Long, narrow cathedral-like windows glow in the wash of my night light. My dining room table gleams like an altar. The high, slanted, open beamed ceiling, the balcony that cradles my office, transmute, turn shadowy as though lit by a dozen candles. A cathedral. Yes. We are in a cathedral. Mimi gags. Tears. A high, keening sound whips around the scarlet stained altar. Screams rip through my throat. Groans. Animal whimpers, yelps.

Hours pass. Little girl arms, tightly wrapped around her teddy bear, are stiff and sore with the effort. I let go the brown cuddly... rub my aching hands, arms. The tension eases. My eyes close.

As the experiences of my alters emerged and were accepted, the amnesiac barrier slowly lifted and we all began to work together. This was a chaotic, frightening time because the memories came pouring out, sometimes tumbling over each other. The pain, grief, and rage were intense and would have been overwhelming if I hadn't been able to use my therapist's office as a container.

For added support, another survivor and I joined with four other women every two weeks. We met for over five years, although eventually cut the meetings down to once a month. We used 12-Step as a framework, telling our stories within the boundaries of the Steps. How life affirming to have our memories, feelings, fears listened to and validated, and to know that arms were always there to hug us when needed.

Integration was not a conscious decision. I would have been happy just to have co-consciousness. But little by little my children started to merge. For them it was both wonderful and frightening. They were no longer alone. They had compassion for each other. On the other hand, they were afraid that integration meant death. In a way, they were correct. It meant they would no longer function as they had for so many years. In compensation, they would be reborn in me, as part of me. For me–the host body–the difficulty was more long lasting. Their feelings and memories became my feelings and memories.

This slow merging process was under way by 1993, when, at my therapist's suggestion, I set aside an hour each evening for my alters to come talk to me. Some evenings no one showed up. More and more, however, we visited and talked. Margery, about twenty-five, let me know that she liked to pick out clothes from the J. Crew catalogue. She loved it when I had my colors done and learned a few simple makeup tricks. Margery was the office worker who had kept us solvent for twenty-five years. Soon, alters would visit me at different hours throughout the day. Not only did my alters visit me, but they eventually communicated among themselves. One night clean, pristine, rigid Naomi, came face-to-face with Ruth (filthy, timid, afraid), and realized the extent of the abuse bundled into this frightened four-year-old. She reached out her arms and scooped Ruth up, holding her tightly against her clean, white blouse. She cried with the pain of Ruth's degradation.

My first encounter with Miriam, Jr., my smart ass, cocky, aggressive alter, was funny—in retrospect. I found myself barking out her name like a drill sergeant. She gave me an "Are you kidding?" look and totally ignored me. A week later I tried again, this time more respectfully. Among other things, I told her I needed her help. She said she would supply it if I got down on my knees and begged for it. It was my turn for an "Are you kidding?" look. I restrained myself and said that I would not get down on my knees and beg. I would, however, get down on my knees and pay tribute to her for her courage, brashness, anger, *chutzpah*. She is the one who did the killing. She is the one who yelled, during a particularly nasty birthday celebration in the cult, where birthdays were special days: "Ruth! Mimi! How can you be so stupid? It's your birthday. We're queen for a day, for heaven's sake. You should be happy. We're up here on a special dais—alive. The other little girls are dead, or will be soon. How can you think we're gonna die? We're too important, too smart to be killed."

I said that I loved her and was grateful to her for bringing us through those years. I stood up and held out my arms. She came to me. I held her while she cried. For the first time, she realized exactly what she had done. Her remorse turned into screams of outrage and pain. I held her until she calmed down.

Soon Miriam, Jr., Ruth, Mimi, Dolly and Naomi merged. It was so gentle that I wasn't aware it had happened until much later, although my world did seem quieter. I frequently felt dizzy, unbalanced. Often I would burst into tears. I attributed these symptoms to the fact that I was frantically working to finish up my Ph.D. Dissertation. It wasn't until my degree was finished and I collapsed and unwound from the stress of the three-and-a-half years, that I felt the grief—acutely—and realized that while my conscious back had been turned, the process of integration had been proceeding.

I also had alters who were programmed by the cult to make the body self-destruct. It was only by the grace of a Higher Power, and hard work, that this did not happen. Maia said that I move with strong spirit. I attempted suicide many times, both directly and indirectly. I wanted to have these alters exorcised. Maia did not say no; she just suggested we wait. We kept the confrontations confined to her office. When their demands and threats were consistently responded to with consciousness and respect, rather than hostility, the cult alters gradually melted into each other. The residue of their essences remains, however. Sometimes it leaks out in the form of denial that the Ritual Abuse happened, denial of my past multiplicity, depression, and an occasional urge to self-destruct. Because this energy is part of me, I can recognize it and work with it more quickly now.

Integration was tough on my body; the memories, the grief and pain were no longer spread over many personalities. They were contained and concentrated in a steadily decreasing number of psyches, and in only one body that now responded to all stimuli. Slowly, however, almost without my being aware of it, I incorporated these alters into my being. One day I noticed the incessant chattering in my head had stopped. Another day when I was promoting a writing class at a university, I realized I was no longer concerned about whether or not pertinent information was available. It was. On yet another day, I had a sense of being three dimensional. I was aware of space all around me. I had always felt flat. Now my body occupied space. The more I integrated, the more I could push out space around me, make it mine, feel safe in it.

I had an increasing array of feelings: pain, joy, fear, exhaustion. When I realized I was custodian of all the feelings and emotions my alters had previously embodied, I wasn't certain I liked the development. It was like having had a maid, a butler, a valet, a chauffeur, a secretary and then waking up one day and finding you have to do all those jobs yourself. I also had flashes of overwhelming loneliness. Never before had I been lonely–for the simple reason that I had never been alone. Despite the fact that my alters are now a part of me, I have felt deep grief at losing their distinct qualities. After all, although I was not consciously aware of them for many years, I knew them intimately. More often, I feel awe, gratitude, great love and affection for the gift of such a remarkable system that contained alters who protected me and brought me through the horrors of my life. Once my alters melted into me, I realized they were all part of the larger me in the same way that I am part of the larger whole.

Now my feelings come from my core, my heart, with no buffering. This leaves me fragile and vulnerable. I have learned, however, to trust that I know who is constant, and who is not, that I know which situations are safe, which are not. Because of this, I am careful about whom I spend time with and how I spend that time. Some of the friends I had in the past, I now know were just acquaintances. I still tend to be reclusive, having just a few friends, but they are close to me. Life is simpler: I don't have to spend forever justifying myself to myself or to others. Because I have more time to relax, feel softer, more compassionate, I can allow people into my world with discretion. I have fewer secrets and barriers, therefore I can be authentic. I am now able to hold my own and stay present in almost any situation.

SPRING 1995

Shed this snake's skin. Enter the world newborn, skin and feelings pink, delicate to the touch. Surrender to pleasure ... yes, pleasure and beauty.

Surrender has always been to pain. I have driven through pain, walked through it, flown through it, crawled through it. Existed. Survived. Surrender has many faces, many facets. Pleasure. How novel. Surrender to pleasure.

I think about that. Surrender to pleasure? Surrender to success? Surrender to a healthy life, guided by love for myself rather than contempt? Can I let go? Can I give up the pain, the misery? Dare I be open to feeling the vulnerability of my new skin, allowing it to age gracefully without the thickening, toughening that comes from the rush to defend? Can I truly surrender?

It has taken time for me to trust that the information, feelings, qualities, and wisdom I need are in me, ready to be tapped. My alters no longer go about their autonomous ways, oblivious of the consequences to the rest of the system. My life is fuller. Until recently, there were times when I found myself calling on a certain alter to help me, then realized that the alter had merged and become part of me.

Some of the physical changes of integration were disconcerting—and wonderful. Colors became sharper, more vivid because my life was no longer veiled. My eyes sometimes blurred, probably because of the coming together of the different alters with their different perceptions, thoughts, ways of seeing. I had a problem—occasionally still do—determining the physical boundaries of my body. I kept bumping into things, feeling unbalanced. My body was a mass of bruises and surface wounds from not properly gauging how it fit into the world around me.

More than any other factor in my healing, the uncovering of my spirituality has been the most valuable. In the past, spirituality was not a word I would have even thought to use. I was aware that music, colors, and nature transported me out of myself, gave me the only surcease from pain and depression I could count on, but I was careful to keep this information to myself for fear of being rebuked or laughed at. I was ashamed of the tears I shed while listening to Berlioz's *Requiem,* or when I first flew over the snowcapped Rocky Mountains at night and imagined the hush that spread over the empty areas between the widely spaced lights.

One spring day in 1994, while listening to Rachmaninoff's *Variations on a Theme by Paganini,* I was flooded by an emotion so deep, I gasped. The tears came—painful, wrenching tears. I remembered that my parents had been communists, materialists:

if they couldn't taste it, hear it, see it, touch it, it didn't exist. The importance for me, however, lies, not in the senses themselves, but in allowing them to unlock my feelings, and then allowing the feelings to connect me with something larger than myself, something outside myself. I call that something the Divine. In earlier days, I would have laughed at the word. My parents had equated spirituality with religion—a crutch, they said, an opiate of the masses—and punished me for any sign or display of "spirituality." I cried, both in remembrance of that past prohibition, and in relief that I was now free to feel and express whatever I needed to feel and express.

Winter 1995

Acceptance. I have been listening all day to Rachmaninoff. Craggy looking man ... thin, narrow face ... prominent nose. He is both sides of the coin ... ascetic looks, plush music. I feel a kinship. Without the sweet heaven of his music, I might have died of despair.

Sergei, you pulled me through the loneliness ... the fire ... the hell ... the exquisite pain of teenage ... and after. You wrapped my sorrows in rich showers of melodies ... stirred my sluggish blood with fingers of gnarled wood that pounded out orgasms of melodies and clashing tones that collided in T. S. Eliot's "small circle of pain" within my skull.

In recent years you softly penetrated my heart, cracked it wide open to experience the Divine ... to know that whatever I lived through was but preparation for the acceptance and joy to come. You lit the way, allowed my tears, softened my edges. Your music sang. I responded.

The possibility that I can open up to this infinite beauty, infinite peace, is astounding. I understand now what the pain is all about: so I can stretch, touch, know the beauty. I feel gratitude. I know that once the pain is worked through—the old pain—I will be left with the capacity to feel the ecstasy. And it will include pain. But pain welcomed as part of life, not inflicted like all the past death, dismemberment, torture.

My body is sweet, aging, hurting—the form in which I live.

I used to think I couldn't carry on a coherent conversation. No one had ever told me that, I just had a sense that my conversation didn't flow easily from Point A to Point B. In thinking back, it probably did flow—I would just blank out periodically and my classroom alter, or another alter would take over. Four or five years ago, while I was working on my Ph.D., I met with a friend who helped me work on the part of my program that dealt with death and dying. Twice a month we had freewheeling discussions about death, dying, my cult experiences, her life experiences (she was eighty at the time), and anything else that seemed pertinent. Fortunately, we taped these discussions. When I played them back, I was aware, for the first time in my life that, even though I didn't recognize the voice as belonging to me, the woman who was speaking was sane, intelligent and not in the least incoherent. Over time, even though I never did come to recognize the voice, I accepted the fact that the words came from me. What a revelation!

I find myself constantly surprised at the depth of my understanding and compassion for others, at my ability to feel touched by another person's grief, to cry in response to another person's pain, rejoice in their joy, and still stay with myself. Because most of my secrets have been uncovered and I have no competing voices in my head, there are fewer barriers between other people and me. I can devote my full attention to them, can really hear what they are saying. This takes energy and, sometimes, I feel tired and drained after being with people.

It took time to narrow my interests. Because I had alters who were outgoing and gregarious, I found myself thinking I could comfortably put myself in the public arena. I couldn't. I had a wealth of ideas and plans left over from the previous occupants. Although I am good at many things, I now know that my pleasure and joy come mainly from the written word, from writing, editing, and channeling people's writing talents so they derive maximum satisfaction and results from their creativity. The knowledge I've learned throughout the years is available to me, even if I still don't remember being in a classroom. Sometimes it slides from my fingertips as though it knows it belongs cradled in the written word.

I am still learning to trust my instincts. Occasionally I wonder why I doggedly pursue certain activities and avenues when they seem to serve no apparent purpose. Rather than feeling guilty, like I used to, I let these passions run their course, finding that they do, indeed, serve a purpose. For instance, I have watched hundreds of videos since 1994, more movies than I knew existed. Because my taste runs to the dark, to the often bizarre, these films have helped me connect with emotions, memories, events that I sometimes have trouble accessing and feeling. On a more practical level, I use films in creative writing workshops, and in my own fiction and nonfiction writing.

If I had any doubts about the integrity of my integration, they were resolved in the spring of 1997 when I had to terminate therapy with my therapist of eleven years; I ran out of money and she could not accommodate my situation. I had desperately hoped to find a way to reverse the money drain. However, none of my plans came to fruition and I became almost penniless. I was in large part responsible for my financial plight: three-and-a-half years of graduate school to get my doctorate; eleven years of expensive therapy twice a week; extensive body work to keep me healthy and connected to my body; stupid and reckless handling of money; miscalculating the amount of time needed to set up my own practice; determination to spend as much time as possible writing.

The timing turned out to be unfortunate. A month after I left therapy, my mother died, disinheriting me. On her death bed, she told my stepbrother—with a smile, he said—that she had no last words to impart to me. The overlapping of these two terminations was almost too painful to bear.

Integration, as I have indicated, was a tough time for me. To have to deal with the final phases of this chaotic time by myself, duplicated my childhood feelings of abandonment and distrust. I was extremely vulnerable, fragile, disoriented, and frequently in tears. Despite my grief, the deepening spirituality that had augmented the work Maia and I did together, provided me a toughness, strength, and resiliency I hadn't thought possible. The integration held. I was able to stay with myself and work through the turmoil. A year later, I began work with another therapist, one more sympathetic to my situation.

I have not been in a romantic relationship since 1991. For many years I did not want one. I had never had what I would call a happy, functional partnership, though I was married twice for an aggregate of thirty years. When I finally felt the desire for a relationship, I knew I had come a long way in working out my childhood abandonment. I was finding in myself the mother love I had never experienced. Dealing with my father's sick, sexualized love of me was more difficult. I had loved my father abjectly—as only an abused child can love the abuser. In all my romantic relationships, I had hooked into a substitute, attempting to get the missing parental love from a partner, a lover, thinking that if I tried hard enough, this time I could make it work.

I bring this up because I had no alters to deflect the enormity of the pain I felt around the lack of healthy parental love and nurturing. It was with me day and night. I finally had to grieve what I had not had the strength to grieve earlier. In time, my father disappeared from my radar screen. I was left with a wasteland, an arid desert that remained from dismantling the fantasies, the substitute lovers, the denial that I had built up to make the truth tolerable—if only barely. I had loved and hated my father with a passion that had outworn its usefulness. I now find myself grateful that I was capable of feeling this tremendous loss so deeply and so directly.

It was only through this process of letting go, that I was able to forgive him for the crimes he had perpetrated against me. I have still to work through forgiveness of my mother, who was involved with the cult. As far as forgiving the cult, all my perpetrators have become dust, a part of that larger whole. Perhaps if I were younger and they were still alive, I might think differently. I might want to find them and take them to trial. I don't know.

Most importantly, have I forgiven myself? I am more tolerant now of my lapses (denial that any abuse happened, workaholism, not taking care of my body), and my imperfections, but there are still parts of my shadow self that I have difficulty bringing into the light of day: rage, aloofness, meanness. Sometimes I think I have forgiven myself, only to find another layer of shame. In the past I said, "I forgive myself." I did so because I thought I should, rather than because I had looked deeply into myself. I came to realize, however, that ten years ago–even six years ago–was too soon to forgive myself, my father, my mother, my stepmother, anyone. I didn't even know the full extent of the crimes. How could I forgive? It is different now. I was a victim then, with no power. Since taking back my power, I have no further need for hatred or revenge.

In 1995, I had a short, simple dream. I was sitting in a restaurant with my father and stepmother. I left the table and when I returned, I looked at my parents for a moment before sitting down again. They looked like two old people, nothing more. I felt no anger, no pain–no charge. When I awoke, having been freed of that terrible love/hate burden, I felt lighter. Forgiveness had been granted me.

The most important thing I have available to the aggregate me is the spirituality I spoke of, the breath of the Divine. Without that sense of something larger than myself, I would not have made it through the eleven years of memory work and depth therapy. I breathed life into my alters over the years, and now they, in turn, have breathed life back into me. Spirituality is the most important thing in my life. My creativity–my writing–comes second, although I cannot really separate them; they are intricately intertwined. For me, the spiritual takes the form of the Feminine Divine, which I have trouble finding words to describe; the Divine does not exist in our time/space continuum. I feel I am a discrete component of something infinitely larger than myself, as is everyone else. In this way, we are all connected, a part of each other because we are all parts of that larger dimension.

A few years ago, I became aware that my process of alter formation duplicated the creative process. In the state during my child's seemingly endless abuse and pain, when the ego could no longer be sustained, it went into eclipse. The flash of creativity happened when the Self leapt into the void trusting she would survive and that a work of art would be born–an alter. I believe this leap into the void could not have happened unless I had had an intuition of a reality larger than myself. It was within this larger divinity that a presence was created to shine light into the dark crevasses of my underworld.

I thought integration followed a linear path: I would become aware of my alters; my alters would relive their experiences; I would become co-conscious with my alters; my alters would merge into each other, then into me; I would be integrated. Period. End. I discovered, however, that my integration, like everything else, followed the Great Wheel of birth, death, rebirth. Alters were born from me. Alters died as separate personalities and became one with me. Every day I undergo a regeneration. Every day there is something new to feel and to learn from the pain of experiencing memories in this body, not in the personalities of split off alters. Every day I must make adjustments to a world that is brimming over with complex relationships and connections. Every day I must confront new situations with the knowledge, wisdom (sometimes the ignorance), the creativity and the love that is a legacy of my alters. Every day I meditate so that I am able to surrender to a quietude deep enough to listen to my inner wisdom. Every day I experience, in a new way, the joy of having my family contained within me rather than split off into amnesiac space. Every day I give and am able to receive. Within this circularity, I can look forward to the process of integration continually unfolding, spiral-like.

JANUARY 1997.

Surrender. Spring pushes the daisies up. . .and I am in Hawaii, on Devastation Trail near Volcano House. Miles of bleached, smooth planks against black lava fields. Nothing to be seen but black and white ... until ... by the side of the trail ... a bright red flower. How it managed to push its way up, I cannot imagine. Small ... but the focus of attention.

Further on another flower ... yellow ... spare ... no leaves ... just a bright yellow flower.

I wonder about my tears at mention of birth/rebirth ... tears of joy, yes, for the beauty of the emergence/reemergence of life ... of color. . . of vitality. But what of the humus out of which birth erupts?

Death. The dead. Black lava fields. Black ... symbol of darkness. Red flower ... splotch of blood upon the desert landscape. Desolation. Are the tears for the desolation ... the aloneness ... the singularity ... the estrangement from all that was meaningful. . . the pain of watching what was once meaningful become banal? It is hard to walk Desolation Trail ... to look back and see your former life fade slowly away. Will my past, like Eurydice, turn into a pillar of salt from my backward glance? Or has it already become a monument accreted from the oceans of tears spilt?

My pain now is this grief of looking back, with adult eyes and presence, at the waste of my life, at the pain of talents never used, never developed. My pen stops. I do not want to continue this clinging to the pain of the past. Time to fill those craters with life present. The lava is not dead ... has never been dead. Blood red flowers ... yellow daisies ... lavender, purple jacaranda ... orange, pink, crimson, scarlet bougainvillea ... white star jasmine ... sprout ... erupt out of the dead years.

I watch my rubber plant push shiny, new leaves out of red sheaths. Did I know what the leaf inside the sheath looked like? No. It was a new experience for me. Did I tear off the sheath in my desire to see what it hid? No. I would have ripped away the developing leaf's protection, nourishment, aborted its young life. Before I write, do I know the content of the embryonic idea within the protecting sheath of my imagination? No.

When the leaves become established, the sheath drops away easily, gladly ... shriveled ... having done its job. Is that what death is like? A dropping away of this shriveled body to make space for the shiny, new entity? And what is that new entity? A soul freed to traverse the spheres? Or perhaps a new way of living ... one that cannot now be imagined?

Be with the mystery, a voice tells me; allow it to unfold in its own time. Surrender to intuition. Surrender to the deep ocean of the unconscious. Be blessed by its waters. Surrender to the divinity of creation.

❧

Terry

173

Lindsey

As I, too, have survived a holocaust of abuse, I have used my healing to help others on their journeys of empowerment and wholeness. On my business bulletin board, I post this quotation by Viktor Frankl, "What is to give light, must endure burning."

My story is centered almost entirely on my journey through integration. As a result, I have only briefly mentioned my history. To share the graphic details was not my focus, nor did it feel important for the purpose of this book. Then, again, not to state the background that lead to my multiplicity, would seem to minimize it. Because of the extreme denial my family and our society have taken to create secrecy about the darkness that has been so prevalent on this planet, it feels important for me to reveal my family history.

When I was seven months in utero, my mother overdosed on barbiturates, almost killing herself, and me as well. After my birth, she stabbed herself and was committed to a famous East Coast university hospital facility. My mother was diagnosed manic-depressive and suicidal. In reality, she was a multiple who spent many of the years during which I lived at home, in psychiatric centers. My sisters, my mother, and I were abused by government doctors experimenting in mind control as well as in viral and genetic research. Many members of my family (on both sides–including my mother, my mother's parents, her brother, and paternal relatives), neighbors, Jewish rabbis, and government officials were Satanists who performed rituals that included bestiality, rape, dismemberment, cannibalism, murder, and prolonged torture with electroshock instruments.

When I was five years old, I died while being tortured. I had a near death experience (NDE), during which I was told by the Beings of Light that I must complete my purpose and be present for the transformation of the planet. The abuse continued until I was twenty-three years old and moved to the West Coast with my husband. We have since divorced. My healing and memories began when I was thirty-five. It has been an incredible adventure.

W*e knew only that we existed to help us survive. We were the ingenuity, the masked cleverness, the breath from mind to voice, aspects of feelings, and children of the depths. We knew how to take control in dangerous times; yet we delighted in play, chatter and amusement. During the merging, how did we know that we, as children, would labor in the birth of an "I." We had watched the body give birth to four children many years before. Nine months—that's how long it took. The ancient meaning of Nine is the end of one cycle, the beginning of a new One. That number was again significant in the time it took us to become one. My name was Anne; I brought forth logical intelligence and detached emotions. From me came Gloria, Andrea, Marianne, Jonathan and Annabel, perhaps more; Lindsey is still learning about the journey of One.*

As each one of us came forward, we got to know each other. That didn't mean we all liked how we did things. It's hard to get along with twenty-eight others and the grown-up. Anne said there was sporadic bickering. Those are big words for me, so I just want to say that we did fight; but we also worked things out, which was most important. Isn't that what happens in a family that really learns to love and care about each other—and take responsibility? It's like dancing; sometimes the rhythm is off, but eventually we get on beat. Oh, yeah ... I was Andrea, the dancer.

I can write from the essences. That is what was left when the We became Me. The Kids—some boys, some girls, one wolf-dog, and an alter who fed submarine sandwiches to her split-off dead part—were the creative gods and goddesses who ruled the survival system of the Lindsey being. It might seem strange to refer to fragmented components of the personality as spiritual icons, yet they knew what I couldn't and didn't understand. They noisily and boldly proclaimed their existence when I could listen. They protected, defended and challenged my memories and sent me on inner journeys to forgotten lands of dark and shadowy terrain. They were real and were charged with the spark of the Creator's presence.

In mythology, the gods and goddesses interacted with mortals, sometimes with reason and logic, often with chaos, and always to challenge them. They explained, through their journeys, the mystery of and reasons for life, and the relationships between people and the Divine. The archetypes existed in me as separate and distinct personalities: they were my gods and goddesses who remain within me as one collective essence of continued accessible support in my inner realms.

It depended on which one of my friends I talked with as to whether I told them I was dissociative ... or multiple. I (always meaning the host personality) usually forgot, and when confronted with my change of labels, would swear I never said I was multiple. How could I seemingly be so highly functional in two professional careers, be a single mother who kept lists of my children's schedules and activities, and never lost time (no amnesiac barriers)? As a gentle reminder that I was working with some kind of separate inside children, I would put on my answering machine, "Hi. You have reached the number for Lindsey and Associates."

From past journals, I found that my writings mentioned the names of several inside kids. Somehow this information did not seem to fully penetrate. It was not until I attended a workshop on multiplicity in August of 1993, that I understood the depth of my dissociation. There, I met many other multiples who experienced co-consciousness, with switching, blending, and alter actions similar to mine.

Theresa, my therapist (not one to use labels or diagnoses), allowed for the wisdom of the body to reveal our truths and listened as I insisted on being called a multiple. To decide to label myself was difficult; yet I felt deep inside that I had to commit to more seriousness about what was happening. In making this shift, fourteen alters surfaced the following year. It was as if, for the first time, the children felt I understood they were *real* and could now present themselves, their truths, and stories.

It was May of 1994. Theresa was helping us deal with a painful and repetitive memory of being pregnant while in the cult. Suddenly, there was a strong, loud interruption from within. This was not Arunda, my Inner Spiritual Mate and Guide[1], whose gentle approach was often present in my sessions and inner life (trance states). It was like a Spiritual Emergency Broadcasting System interrupting a dramatic soap opera for an important announcement. The memory stopped and a voice of deep resonating power spoke, "Let in Love. It's about knowing your innocence and claiming each piece of yourself, no matter how small. Every piece has to be reclaimed and honored. Every piece is precious. It is the energy, frequency, and vibration of GOD; and you do *not* know it!"

All the kids were watching far behind the eyes, set deep within a reclusive space of the body. A feeling of surging energy exploded inside. They took cover deeper within, leaving our body and the adult self to feel the intensely overwhelming emotional shock, as lifetime after lifetime sped through my consciousness. It was if I was viewing a VCR in fast rewind, feeling as if I was part of the drama on the tape.

Is this what happens when you die?! I remember reading in books and articles on death and dying, on near death experiences, about how people must review their lives at death. But I

---

[1] *Inner Spiritual Mate*: a deeply loving Guide similar to spiritual anima/animus. *Guide*: spiritual being who compassionately and wisely assists my process.

was still in physical reality, and I was viewing and reviewing lifetimes. The guttural sobs of collective remembrances poured through every cell of my being.

Through the mass confusion and fear, a *spark of inner awareness* surfaced. I spoke it out loud to Theresa, not understanding what I was saying. I had a vague recognition that each alter/dissociation of myself in this lifetime represented unclaimed or disconnected parts of myself in other lifetimes. To expand that reality, the people/players of those past lifetime dramas who acted with me, mirrored the adversity, discord and unexpressed feelings that I now embodied as alters. My system of fragmented survival in the present included all the parts that I had not resolved from the past. And I had just experienced all of this in the Now.

I cried until I could remember to notice my breath. I was alive. I hadn't died. Why? Why now? That *spark of inner awareness* was the first impulse of a new view of life. Is this how life begins—with a cosmic impulse from energy into form? I knew somewhere in my core, deep in my soul, that I had to experience this to give birth to my wholeness. In choosing this traumatic life, I created a means to reconnect with myself at the deepest levels.

Theresa, with the clarity and groundedness of an ancient seer, viewed my experience as a cluster of stars whose coming together would form a super nova, whose light would become even stronger and brighter.

Because of my fractionated personalities and abuse memories, life took on a dreamlike quality—a waking dream. Time became mystical; it collapsed into one moment and/or expanded into many realities.

It is within this nonlinear context that my Spiritual Guides act. As my Higher (not Highest) Power, they guide me to experiences that enable me to access life's deeper meanings. In this way, I can incorporate knowledge and wisdom from many different philosophies: mythology, shamanism, Judaism, Christianity, Eastern and New Age thought.

D*ivine Impulse ... spark of awareness ... energy ... thought ... form (impregnation) ... birth.* I've often pondered about this pattern of Creation and the ways it manifests. Could I have known that this *spark* or *Divine Impulse* was to bring forth the Tantric or sexual energy needed to seed my body and being with a new thought—to give birth to just one ME?

Tantra energy can express itself in many ways. When the fertile time of my cycle arrives, my body naturally awaits its seed by wanting to be sexually expressive (not a great birth control method if I act it out physically). So I ride with the waves of the feeling. For me, as a woman, this has to do with my feelings of receptivity and longing—to let life in, to let love in. My fertile creations arouse me with energy to fuel more flowing thoughts, ideas, projects or inner journeys. Often these feelings become obscured and nebulous when the fertile cycle wanes.

By July of '94, my sexuality had been reawakened through dating several men. Leah, my shamanic healer[2], knowing that these issues of sexuality had been stimulated, wanted to help me create a female role model different from the ones on which this dysfunctional society is based. I was to find a female ancestor.

Going deep inside, I traveled to the time of the Great Pillars, the time of the sacrifice of animals to the triple Goddess Diana. The ancestor was not there.

"Go even deeper, further within until you connect with her." Leah's voice drifted gently into my trance state.

The desert was dotted with periodic risings of barren mountains. Within the mountains were caves of great immensity. I knew this area well, as I had traveled to it with my family and tribe each year. It was Now time, and this year I would participate. This year was my initiation into manhood. With girls and boys of my same age, we carefully climbed the mountain led by the initiated from the year before. The boys continued to travel several hundred feet higher to be lead one by one into the upper caves—the masculine ... sky ... air ... intellect ... ascending. The girls were sent to the lower caves—the feminine ... earth ... intelligence ... descending ... depth. In the upper cave of darkness, I sat

[2] *Shamanic Healer:* a person who practices the spiritual customs of visionary experience and revelation central to many ancient indigenous cultures.

calmly for many hours. Then the voices came, and could be distin-
guished as the movement of three winds across my face. My mind gradu-
ally altered the experience into evolving shapes that solidified into pic-
tures of a girl, Lindsey, looking at her mother's book, East of the Sun,
West of the Moon, *with its stories of the winds. The voices said they*
appeared as the three winds so that Lindsey's fear of her once abusive
mother would not be associated with the Feminine.

The past had just merged into the present. The Indian boy of the past "me" saw his future self, and I witnessed a past life self. Time became the Now, in the present, as the ancestral winds explained they had been waiting a long time to help me, to be there for me. To remember this meeting and to support my healing, I was to take my right middle finger and place it between the middle and index fingers of the left hand. This action makes a whole connection, like a plug in an outlet or a penis in a vagina: it is the symbol for completeness in sexuality and union.

The ancients understood the number Three to be the birthplace of Creation. The triple goddess Diana, the three ancestral winds, the three fingers, and existing within me, my three Lucys, the three-in-one alters of dark sensuality, sexuality and passion—how perfectly the pieces fit.

D*iscovery of deep sexual overtones, revealed through the synchronicity of memories and outside events, is starting to seep further in as I write about my integration.*

I was attracted to Todd, a biologist, in August of 1994. We were walking playfully around a lake when he wandered into a high grassy area near the water's edge to look for frogs. My emotions became triggered as I realized that the natural predators of frogs are snakes. My immense fear of snakes tightened my body. Taking this intense feeling into therapy, I remembered the cult photographing a ritual where a snake was allowed to bite a small, helpless baby to death. I wanted to interpret this horror as being symbolic, as phallic or the rising of *kundalini energy*[3], but this memory was quite real. The body does not lie. I was afraid that the memory would continue with

---

[3]*Kundalini energy*: life force energy that ascends from the coccyx through the head.

the snake being used to terrorize me as the cult had done at other times. This did not happen. What followed was a spontaneous metaphoric experience. A weird image of a Hopi Katchina doll appeared coming out of my vagina in shades of blood red representing the release of love and passion. I was birthing a symbol of "fertile growth," and the birth was devoid of labor pains as the Katchina flowed freely out of me.

As the Earth has received the monthly bloods of Indian women to fertilize their crops, letting go can create fertile growth that supplies nourishment and groundedness. When the ground produces, the tribes must harvest and partake of its bounty so that they may receive in return. To let go and to receive is a cyclic awareness of the flow of love and life.

I felt that receiving love and releasing the dark memories were always going to be painful because of the extreme abuse I experienced in my childhood. But a shift had occurred through this symbolic reframing, and my sexuality, as an integral part of the birthing process, took on a deeper meaning.

L ife is a mirror. Obviously I'm not the first person to realize this. It's just that the mirror is too often in my face. Everything that triggers me on the outside is an opportunity (on my enlightened days) to go within. It's certainly no joy ride to remember the split off memories, but neither is the way the body retains the cellular pain/memory. I know my body's language when it wants my attention. Pain works effectively. Suffering is hanging out with pain too long, thinking it might go away, and resisting going inside myself. When there are scared kids within who are having the pain/feelings/memories, life can be intense.

The triggers are more quickly activated when the opposite sex is involved, as I discovered when Jack answered my personal dating ad (*No, we weren't desperate. It's a nineties thing*). He was a psychiatric nurse (*red flags waving, system alert!*). I asked him about his work. He had on occasion worked with multiples (*we later found out mostly by medicating them*). He wanted to work more with them. (*We thought we should meet him.*)

I tried not to let his baldness bother me, but the kids were running danger signals throughout the body. The beard was attractive, though. I really like beards. I was clear that there was no romantic connection, but I accepted an invitation to meet with him a second time.

He had shaved his beard. The baldness was more predominant. The kids kept thinking about his appearance being similar to our bald Grandfather (perpetrator), and I sensed he had money issues that reminded me of my dad. The trigger was activated. The Universe had "innocently" synchronized the process. The nurse man's true function was only to stimulate the reflection, and the reflection carried me inside.

The memory was about being held down and raped by my grandfather, by a government doctor and by my mother when I was five. My quiet, hopeless five-year-old alter, Karan, was ready to leave the body and die. Jonathan, my tough, rebellious inner teenager, rescued her by attempting to fight off the perpetrators. He was very angry that he had to rescue the body again, and that he never had help from the other older alters in rescuing the little ones. Jonathan was sending warning signals not to go out with the nurse man. He felt overwhelmed with responsibilities from both past and present experiences.

With Theresa's mediation, several Guides and our totem dragon[4] volunteered to take over his responsibilities, if Jonathan would ask them to help. He would then be free to do what he wanted to do. Jonathan cried with disbelief. Could he trust them? It was always him, by himself. Of course, he didn't ask for help! How could he? He was created to save the system.

Freedom! Yes, he wanted to ride off on a motorcycle like James Dean, Marlon Brando, and Peter Fonda. He would use a dragon symbol (dragons incinerate dangerous people) on his helmet and be known as the Dragons Out Of Hell instead of Hell's Angels. He would ride into the woods.

Jonathan was excited with the new role change. He had learned several months earlier about chopping trees to deal with his anger and decided to use the felled trees in the woods as a means to build a community log cabin for the kids. It would

---

[4] *Totem dragon*: in shamanic tradition, a creature or animal energy that is called upon for support or aid.

start with a store, the bottom floor for an ice cream and candy facility and the upstairs rooms for space, safety, and games.

I thought life had settled down until a few days later. Severe grief overtook my body. The younger kids were devastated. How could Jonathan just take off and leave them? He had to be part of the family. What did he mean by just taking off?

It felt as if he was trying to further dissociate from everyone inside. There was a sense of ungroundedness. Theresa didn't see his leaving as permanent, especially if he was planning to build a cabin for the kids. He definitely needed space just for himself.

While discussing this situation in therapy, a terrible pain above my right eyebrow, like a tearing feeling, suddenly emerged and Jonathan came forward. He brought forth a memory with him. The little ones, maybe two or three years old, had witnessed a murder that was too horrifying for them— a man was dismembered while still alive. They screamed for help, for themselves, for the man who was killed. In a whirl-pool of massive, dark chaos, a tough, strong, angry Jonathan had formed. Through this black formless space, from the internal tear above my right eyebrow, he was created to help them and, at the same time, another energy attached onto Jonathan. The dead man's spirit heard the cries of the little ones and wanted to help them. The entity had felt it couldn't move into the Light, so it entered Jonathan to help save the Lindsey body. Although Jonathan was not aware that he carried the entity within him, the little ones knew that it had been helping them all those years as well. That explained their desperation and feelings of abandonment. Since Jonathan's rescue job had been renegotiated and delegated to the Guides, the entity's work was no longer necessary either. Jonathan needed to be free in a new way. It was time to release the man's spirit back into the Light.

The entity was afraid to leave the body and enter the Light because he believed he would be punished for originally participating in the cult. Theresa gently explained that, for all those years, he had helped to protect the little ones and save the body. He would surely be welcomed into the Light. We cried, particularly the little ones, as two beings of Light helped him exit the crown chakra[5] and return his spirit to its rightful source. More energy would be available for the system, and Jonathan could be fully himself.

It was getting close to Halloween (1994). "Generic" Satanists celebrate this holiday on October 31 or November 1 with rituals of torture and murder. Jewish Satanists[6] must go by a different calendar because I remember the holiday being quite fun with school costume parties and neighborhood trick or treat walks. The inside kids and I weren't in panic at this time. It was usually several weeks before and after that the switching and memories appeared as a sign that rituals had occurred.

My three teenage Lucys had emerged in a "Jewish Halloween" memory as being prepared by the cult women to marry the "Prince[7]." In their struggle to resist, measures were used to restrain them and make all the alters forget by applying electroshock torture. The scar I had always wondered about on the right side of my belly, told its story as a burn mark made by a cattle prod during this ritual.

Arunda's soothing, etheric voice gently took over the memory to explain that with the emergence of Fall (a dual metaphor for the fall of denial and the time of year), and a change in seasons, comes a change in life. It was time to look at the overview of our process in seeing how far we had traveled in our healing: knowing who was involved, what happened so far, how the body talked, who lived inside, programming and thought forms. The whole process depended upon my willingness to reexperience what I didn't want to feel and remember. Was I ready to allow myself (and the rest of the children) to be open to receive the information and healing for the next level in my life?

What did this mean? The fear of the word *integration* started

[5]*Crown chakra*: in the seven energy fields of the body, the top of the head.

[6]*Jewish Satanists*: In the cult that I was involved in, the perpetrators' masked religion (shown publicly) was of the Jewish religion. Ironically, Jews do not believe in Satan which makes it harder for the abused to be believed.

[7]*"The Prince"*: referring to Satan or Lucifer.

to bubble up to the surface, yet with Arunda directly communicating with us this fear stayed buffered. *We won't think about that "word" that means ... death; and we won't listen anymore if Arunda says "it!"*

"It is her choice if she (Lindsey) wants her parts to come into unification. There is a core personality deep within her, an essence that exists."

He heard our thoughts even as we tried to hide them from him; but we're glad he didn't use "that word!" We know each other only as "We." Change always happens, so we're not going to worry what he means by "unification."

By mid-November, Jonathan's large log cabin was almost completed. The downstairs had not had its soda fountain and ice cream parlor working, but everything in due time. Jonathan's simplicity of design allowed for much creativity in its use. If one of the kids needed his/her own space to just be alone, or talk privately to the adult functioning part, a room was set aside.

I had watched the movie, *Crooklyn*, with two of my outer children. The movie was about a struggling Afro-American family in Brooklyn, and there were multiple scenes of physical child abuse. Within a few days, I started to feel cold symptoms. This meant I must check within immediately. Annabel, nine, wanted to be acknowledged and nurtured after remembering how "mother with the wild eyes" had beaten her. As she rested in one of the upstairs rooms of the cabin, she would cough often to remind me to check in on her. When she got bored, she invited Lisa, four, to a tea party, and played Barbie dolls with Marianne, eleven. Everyone participated in enjoying the containment of their new home in the recesses of our body.

My continuing issues around hair loss have pushed me in many different directions to seek answers. The shame that always arises goes through spirals where my self-esteem deflates, and I then feel immobilized, ugly, hopeless and powerless. It's as if the world can see my wounds. In not wanting to perpetuate my victimhood for too long (though the feelings have often been overwhelming), I will pull together my courage and journey to whatever memory or alter holds the feelings, or use whatever energy healing modality or nutritional alternative seems workable.

In late November 1994, I was sharing my hair loss issue with an acquaintance at a dance class. She happened to be a nutritional counselor. A close friend of hers, a psychic nutritional healer, was coming to visit. There are no coincidences. I scheduled an appointment with her friend in December.

Christine was an attractive woman in her forties. Her deep set blue eyes—with the intensity to penetrate a thick concrete wall—made me think she would know how to take charge and help me. But then, of course, I wasn't going to turn the process over to her just like that. I tested her ability to hear me, be grounded and communicate honestly. I briefly explained to her about my childhood abuse issues and the existence of the kids inside. Generally I don't fully trust the clarity and boundaries of psychics, so I knew I would have to use discretion in hearing what she told me.

What We, and I say We as the whole system, experienced were two hours of incredibly intense entity removal—over ninety-five disincarnate spirits. The body was going through pain. Strong waves of grief and fear arose as clusters of entities were thrust out. Christine was calling forth the Ascended Masters[8], swooping a real sword around my body to cut the etheric cords[9] of connections to them. I was going through memory after memory. The entities were hiding inside the alters as well as the body. I finally told her I had had enough! She insisted there were more.

"You know, Rome wasn't built in a day!" I gasped, as another wave of pain tried to move through. "This is a process, not a happening, and I've had enough!" I asserted my boundaries and it felt powerful to take care of everyone inside. I left rather spacey with feelings that shifted from peacefulness to

[8]*Ascended Masters*: high level energy beings who once inhabited form and aid in the raising of consciousness on Earth.

[9]*Etheric cords*: nonmaterial, psychic energy particles that connect from person to person, animal or object that create the loss of power.

emotional release.

When I checked in with the kids at therapy the following week, they were looking cautiously out the windows of their log house not wanting to come out. *What if that sorceress is around? She is like Merlin: not bad, just too serious, on a mission.* They had become frightened and upset with Christine when they heard her say that multiplicity had more to do with entity attachments and demonic possessions than full ego splits. She did not think "I" was as fractionated as I thought. I assured the kids that I was not going to try to integrate. We were really getting to know and work with each other, and I was happy with this arrangement.

The kids knew that I wanted to see Christine again to remove what she referred to as the "rest of the entities" and make sure the hair loss stabilized. "We don't want to let go so fast!" I asked them why they were hiding those other beings inside them. "We can't tell you everything at once."

"But I don't want to continually lose my hair!" As I spoke those words, a rageful voice, not of my system, screamed defaming remarks at me. I knew an entity removal was necessary (and I could do it myself since I had training as a hypnotherapist), but I had to know why it existed in me first. This energy had come into Rachel, thirteen, who had been so severely tortured that she could never speak without having long pauses between each word. I realized why the kids could not reveal what they knew about the entities inside themselves—it was physically and emotionally difficult for all of us to go through the trauma of remembering too quickly. This multilevel process had started with the entity removal in Jonathan and was continuing at its own pace.

In meditation that week, the Inner Guides said there was going to be an earthquake between mid to late January 1995. I was taking a financial course and decided, as my project, to research and buy homeowner's insurance that included earthquake coverage. My insurance agent was intrigued that I had an intuitive hit about a possible earthquake.

(Koji, Japan was hit by a devastating earthquake on January

17. It was part of the circular fault line that had created havoc in Los Angeles the year before, and the same fault circle that involved my area. My insurance agent was impressed with the prediction, but glad it had not hit our area.)

More changes were subtly occurring of which I was not fully aware at the time. I experienced a shift in therapy about judging myself and others and allowing myself to receive and let in love. In my waking state, I noticed that my protected heart was opening more. This produced feelings of layered grief that were strangely nebulous. It was like a new concept being introduced. It would quickly flash into consciousness, not quite long enough to grasp it. I had to experience it repeatedly to integrate the new ideas or feelings. These new, foreign feelings were difficult to hang out with. Were they mine, the functional adult–or the kids? This experience of shifting appeared in my dream state as coming apart at the center of my head.

It was hours away from New Year's when my throat signaled me by getting sore. As I allowed myself to sink into a mire of undefined sobs, it would release and clear. Something big was happening; I had to "be" in the unknown. This was not my favorite comfort zone but what other choice did I have?

On my forty-third birthday, mid-January of 1995, I went into a deep, two-day depression. Of course, with my background, that would seem par for the course except it had not happened in a long time. This felt very different. My neck reacted by stiffening. It took five hours of using energy/body work on myself to loosen it up. The attitudes/depression then shifted.

My therapy session on January 20 dealt with an awareness of a group reorganization inside–an incorporation. With so many entities removed, the kids were no longer responsible for hiding or caring for those incarnate spirits. The question came from the kids concerning responsibilities within the system, "Who are we, and what are we supposed to do now that things have changed?" Without consciously communicating their answers, they tightened their bond with each other, moved closer to the front of the body, and started speaking collectively to me rather then individually. Somehow, they seemed more trusting of the adult functional part of me to be their spokesperson. In this way, they would not have to "come out" as much by using the mind and body as they used to. They seemed much happier, less burdened. And I was deeply concerned!

What if they reorganized again without telling me, without knowing? What if they integrated?! What if there were no voices for me to talk to, to laugh or cry with? I would be lost!

The thoughts passed as I checked deeply inside. Yes, the kids were still audible, but different. Two of the girls, Lisa, four, and Alicesad, eight, once visually blurred and vague to my inner sight, appeared clearer with details I never sensed before. The fear arose again. Are they showing up this way before they leave me? I was starting to panic. I let Theresa guide me within so that I could allow myself the feelings and awareness of being safe with the dark unknown.

T he kids let me know that they were scared to see Christine on January 26, but would be brave anyway. They *knew* we had to do this work, that *we didn't want what is not part of us, inside us.* As I listened to them, I saw a vision of Moses taking his once scattered flock of survivors across the Red Sea, trusting the separation of the sea to save them, and finally reorganizing on the other shore.

C hristine came to my home, to my healing room, to remove the entities. The Lindsey system was nervous, yet outwardly calm. I knew Christine's procedure, but her energy seemed more intentional. After removing six to eight low level demonic energies (her description probably referred to the energies' destructive nature) in different chakras[10], she directly said my inner people were demons posing as children even though there was some fragmentation from the abuse.

As open as I tried to be, her statement was not settling well. How could I have done as much healing and learned to reparent myself without my kids' keen perceptions, memories,

[10] *Chakras*: energy centers within and around the body.

cooperation and incredibly rich personalities? No! A mother knows her children, and they could not be demons!

When Christine asked to remove those "demons," I explained that if I decided in the future to allow that, I needed to make closure first. I had learned to love each of them. It was an important decision to stay with my gut reaction, and yet Christine's perception almost filtered through and became mine. In the meantime, I chose to use the Ascended Masters' decrees (channeled words from high vibratory, spiritual beings) to release anything that was not of or from me and was not serving my highest purpose.

Two days later at a dance convention, I took a nurturing break in my hotel room. As I flung my aching body into warm bath water, I reconnected with two of the kids. Margaret, six, with her sweet, blunt and narcissistic wit spoke first, "I want my thick red hair. Anything that doesn't let me have it, take it out of me! You know that Christine lady is very weird. You don't think we're demons, do you?" Without directly answering her, I assured her that I loved her and that would always be true.

Annabel, nine, came forward after Margaret felt acknowledged. "All of US kids need to talk and make a decision together. We know that lady thinks we're demons. Maybe she scared you into thinking that part of us are like that. We don't want something inside us that isn't us. We'll have to see what to do together. I will cough next Saturday to get your attention so you will know we have decided what to do. Make sure you remember to listen."

Annabel knew me so well. I had started to doubt myself, my healing journey and the truths I knew were mine. In the two days after Christine's visit, I attempted to hide my obsessive thoughts about demons and entities possessing everything and everybody, from the kids and myself. Even trusting my Guides became difficult. I had let my power leech and allowed Christine's "sight" to filter into mine.

I coughed a few times Saturday night. I was almost asleep. Having just been to a friend's birthday and also having dealt with my outer children that weekend, I was too tired to respond to the cough.

My eyes blurred quite often during the following week with occasional bouts of dryness, as if they had a film over them and were unable to tear. I thought that my body was responding to the January reorganization, with the kids not using the eyes in the same way. I did not take the time to really listen or call out to them until I slowed down to do my journal writing on Wednesday.

Feeling very tired, unmotivated, confusion, fear. Is this the way an incorporation progresses? They're still with me. I KNOW they are ... yet it feels as if they're not around! Am I numb, not hearing and feeling them out of fear of what Christine said about them?

The next morning (February 9), I called out to them before work.

Silence.

"Oh God! Where are they?!" I had to stop the swelling of tears since it was essential to wear my professional mask at work. I didn't know how I would keep things together that day.

In the evening, by no coincidence, I went to a lecture to hear Shakti Gawain, author of *Path of Transformation*. One of the meditative exercises was to listen to my inner guidance. Oh yeah. I hadn't listened to Arunda during the week. As I dropped within, he gently acknowledged, "In your reorganization, know you are loved and it will bring you to a higher state of integrity." I thought about that word. Integrity means to become whole. Did Arunda mean this reorganization was about INTEGRATION?

I called inside to the kids again the next morning. No one answered! I went through all their names individually–Lisa, Jason, Maureen, Daphne–on and on.

Nothing!

Bursting forth, a collective sound of "WE are YOU" resonated ... then silence ... so dark and empty.

I was immersed in sheer panic and terror! I could hardly drive myself to therapy that morning. My eyes were not close to being dry now.

"'They're GONE!" I screamed until I could hardly breathe. "They didn't say GOOD-BYE! They made the decision without telling me! I forgot to listen! I decreed too much! I thought it was to remove whatever wasn't part of us to go into the Light! Where are my kids?!"

I was in shock. It took Theresa most of the session to anchor me in my body. It was when she had me draw the feelings from inside, that I experienced a sense of groundedness. I first drew separate, individualized stick children with space between them, all in a container that fit within my whole body. Next to it, I drew another container with squiggly lines all through it—there was no space between them, like a contained melting pot of energy, an essence.

In a moment of insight, Theresa suggested that perhaps the decrees of releasing what wasn't of the system, removed the space between the children that had originally kept them separated. Once that was released, they merged.

Yes. Somehow, that perception felt right and very painful. It was too fast. It felt as if twenty-eight children died, my children! How would I come to grips with being left in this world by myself? My feelings, and who I had been, were filtered and expressed through these kids. I grew to trust their funny stories and hidden and terrifying truths.

I could say "Alicemad doesn't want to do that," or, "Maureen was feeling that way." To realize that I must take one hundred percent responsibility for my actions, was so exposing. I felt naked, like a newborn. I would *have to* live in the mystery of creating myself in a new way, and allow time, in all its dimensions, to show me. Just as it took nine months to birth each of my four outer children, it had taken nine months to birth myself.

I went through February feeling like I had when I separated from my husband five years earlier—surges of overwhelming grief and anger. I blamed it on Christine and on myself for staying in denial about the process. I wondered what I could have done differently.

During my periods of peacefulness, especially in meditation, I was astonished at the lack of static and the ease with which I heard the communications with Arunda and my other Guides. In my outer conversations, I started to listen differently, not being triggered or dissociated. My perceptions of what I thought were people's intentions changed as I stayed present in myself. The subpersonalities–the judge, the critic, etc.–were active but in a gentle way. The part of me that just watched this unfolding was definitely ME.

I visited Leah in mid-March to do more shamanic work. In telling her about my process around the earthquake and the insurance I bought (which was canceled around the time of my integration due to my area's earthquake ratings), she brought a new light to my Guides' message about an earthquake occurring.

An earthquake is often a cataclysmic experience that involves huge earth movements. Foundations can crumble, structures collapse, people go through power shifts as their emotions are fueled in survival. Is that not what I experienced? The insurance represented not an outside policy, but a supportive and loving internal "insurance" and connection with my guidance and process. A quake had definitely happened–inside me.

In telling Leah about Christine's perception of my kids as demons, Leah sensed a deep level of fear within me. Going into a trance state with her Guides, she saw the children as a collective essence existing outside my body consciousness. They were in shock from the removal of the space and from being in a new form. The kids expressed a strong desire to live in Jonathan's house in the woods within me. Did I still think they might be demons? They wanted me to know that they were NOT demonic and didn't want me to ever think that! They were not going to come back in the old form because they knew I had to grow up. Would I still love and remember them?

I sobbed. I had never stopped loving them for one moment. Just to have this communication with them, to know that they hadn't dissolved into nothingness, brought up feelings of bittersweet joy inside me. To hell with the demons! Yes, I wanted them to be in the House of Jonathan, living in essence as One. They would never be gone, just be in a different form, inside me. This was such a tremendous relief and release to the overwhelming grief I was experiencing.

"Was there anything else they needed from me?" I wanted to keep the dialogue going. It had been so long. Inside myself, I heard *flowers*–a sign of Earth in its beauty. I dedicated my little backyard garden to them with an angel birdbath as their guardian. My lush azalea bush, with its delicate red flowers that bloom in February, would become the E.O.C. bush–the Essence of Children bush. Now they would have a place where they were honored, loved and remembered, outside and inside me.

Bringing the children's collective essences inside my body (through the soul retrieval), where Jonathan's house existed, was a turning point. The feelings of grieving the old form continued for another six months. Learning how to take baby steps in letting in and accepting my *own* feelings and experiences is still a process. But *time*, in its gentleness, by giving space, assists such transitions.

Like Dorothy in the Wizard of Oz, who had to take a long and mysterious journey–sometimes delightful, more often frightening and courageous–to find herself, I, too, have traveled the paths of the unknown to connect with Me. To deeply embrace the concept that "there is no place like home," becomes my metaphor for remembering I can always come back to myself, my spiritual embodied home, no matter where the journey takes me now.

Over three years have passed since 1995 when We became Me. Integration does not seem like the finality my alters once thought it was. Not that I think for one moment that I will separate into distinct people. It seems clear that I will stay ME, and I don't wish it any other way. Integration–becoming whole–is my continuing process into the mystery of my life's unfoldment. I will always integrate new outer and inner experiences: thoughts, emotions, shadow (hidden) or subpersonality characters, memories, and relationships. But all of this is Me, and I am solely responsible for how I work with, and take action in this process.

Soon after the complete reorganization and integration, I started working with my body, as I would with the inner people. Since I didn't quite know how to connect with myself, I would ask what the painful parts were saying. In other words, I gave voice to my body parts, let them dialogue with each other, then refereed and allowed for negotiation. I knew this worked in connecting with my feelings because the pain would dissipate immediately afterwards.

Within three months, I identified an "inner child" that existed inside me, a three-year-old part that looked like me at that age, and whose energy did not feel fractionated from the core of me. I knew that she was not an alter. As I lovingly parented and gently listened to her, memories eventually surfaced. It surprised me at first. My Guides had said that I had more memories but they would be processed differently. I wanted to think this wasn't true because I was enjoying the respite from "memory lane" and hoped I was past that stage. Why couldn't I just deal with feelings? Nonetheless, I experienced terror as the body's pains shifted from feelings into memories. I had never done memories by myself, without alters!

This became my test. The memories progressed from the half forgotten early incest to ritual abuse scenes. The intensity of the memories brought me to the point of remembering again how the alters were initially formed. Above my right eyebrow, I felt the tearing, the darkness, the void. Would I split again or was I experiencing how I used to split? It was almost as if I had a choice whether or not to call an alter out of Jonathan's house. The Guides said I did have a choice and congratulated me for being courageous in feeling the memory myself. "This is the way you must learn to be strong as one. No matter whether a situation is perceived as good or threatening, you must learn to stay clear and present as one."

Dissociation is different for me now. I believe that as humans, we all dissociate in degrees, from zoning out with TV to forgetting where we place things. As a multiple, the degrees are much greater. The children in my system (separate from the core personality that I didn't know I had at the time) had carried the feelings of the past into the present. Triggering events, situations, or conversations would often lead to panic, severe switching, body imbalance, physical pain and abreaction (identification with being in the past in unconscious memories). I, as the host, had the ability to witness the past occurrences with some detachment, but this was still scary. I often resisted doing memory or feeling work until the body pain or dissociation forced me inside.

I now identify the triggers/memories as events that allow me to claim my forgotten history, power, feelings and wisdom. I experience the memories in multidimensional time shifts. The present, Now time, gives me the trigger, the spark, to view the past by experiencing it as if it was happening in the past, or viewing it from the present, with the ability to shift gears. This is similar to abreacting but with full conscious ability to move to the present at any point. My detached adult part can also observe myself as the once child/alter having the feelings and trauma (*e.g.,* Dorthea is pushing Poppy away, crying and screaming), or the adult part of me can access the feelings with the awareness that it is me, the adult remembering and feeling as a child (*e.g.,* I was ten and so scared when Uncle Bob held me down). All three states can shift and blend during the remembering. These are understood within me as interwoven, timeless shifts. The experience still isn't a fun house, but the richness of the inner work and the revelation of the truth in synchronistic manifestations of the outer world (what happens in my inner world shows up in my outer world) is quite incredible.

Although my inner people exist only in essence, I can remember their feelings and what they knew and held for me in this new way. This brings comfort when I feel lonely, a new feeling since the integration. With all those kids chattering inside, how did I know about "lonely?"

I'm used to doing this work alone now, sometimes without

my therapist, in the safety of my meditation cushions. I realize I am never alone on this journey. The clarity with which I can hear my Guidance has increased my sense of focus and purpose. I know that our communications keep me alert, heard, and protected.

I have experienced some physical changes since the integration (besides the fact that I am several years older). Although I did not wear glasses as an adult, my eyes seemed to become increasingly farsighted soon after the shift. I'm not sure if my inner kids kept my eyesight young and stabilized prior to integration. Perhaps the trauma of the integration stressed my outer sight. I find, now, that I have to use glasses to read small print—not one of the advantages of being a singleton (one of the terms I use to describe my oneness).

My personal energy level has increased, although how I use it is more focused and less chaotic. Before, I needed more activities and people outside my home to feel energized. I'm still socially active, but I enjoy more time by myself, without friends or family.

Having an adult conversation, without being taken over by a twelve-year-old, is definitely easier and less humiliating in social settings. So often in the past, I couldn't believe what I heard come out of my mouth, and there wasn't a thing I could say to rectify it because I wasn't the one using the body. When a friend, with a strong sense of motherhood, noticed that my sassy, pre-pubescent Andrea had the car keys and was going to attempt to drive us home from a dance, the atmosphere became confrontational. It took much longer to get home. I'm glad to say that making decisions in my life now feels sane and coordinates with the situations I'm in.

I haven't lost the childlike innocence, kid playfulness, or teenage rebel attitude that were once held by individual alters. These states are recognized by energy shifts of feeling rather then entire personalities, but they are Me. The feeling of neediness that was so accessible in my younger alters is still difficult to allow into consciousness and to feel gentle acceptance for. It's a process and I continue to work with it.

My outer children now have a mother who is present for them. I no longer get hysterical when they teasingly throw my teddy bear across my bedroom. I don't yank the phone away and hang up on them when my six-year-old alter doesn't like the conversation. There is predictability in my behavior.

With the integration, came the recognition of the many gifts and lessons that were brought to fruition. I can see my life beyond the dramas and the traumas that occurred. My intuition became sharper and continues to deepen. Evolving from being many to one took massive creative ingenuity from the formation to the transformation. This evolution is an expression of a deep soul love and divine purpose. In learning to love all my personalities, I have the ability to know great compassion for myself and for others. Even the darker aspects of my persona are welcomed and embraced into my process. I need all of me to be Me, to be whole, to be ONE.

With compassion comes a release into forgiveness. Forgiveness is such a misunderstood word. Parts of me were culturally programmed with "if you apologize or forgive, then everything is better and you can forget the hurt, the injustice, the abuse and move on in your life." The fact that old entrenched, dysfunctional patterns don't heal or change with "I'm sorry," or "I forgive you," was not taken into consideration. Those words are really the antithesis of the true awareness of forgiveness. Shakti Gawain, noted author and speaker articulates that, "Forgiveness occurs when we have completed the learning process of a particular experience and are ready to release it and move on. If we rush to forgive before we are ready, we may short-circuit our own learning process, repress our other feelings and miss an opportunity for greater healing." Thus forgiveness is really just an aspect of the whole process of healing, not a means to an end.

I define forgiveness as a state of Grace whereby charged, tumultuous feelings that once connected me to another person or situation, totally disengage or disconnect with compassion. Through attentive insight, I have sensed the charge as psychic/

energy cords that I would not cut or unplug even though they continuously fed my feelings and power to someone else. In this charged state, my deceptive belief system thinks it has an investment to stay connected, even though the leeching drains me and can feed those who abused me. It's not a process that occurs cognitively. It's not rational. In being willing to recognize my part, Grace, in its divine timing, manifests the impulse to truly cut loose, release, allowing me to reclaim myself and my power.

Have I gone through "forgiveness?" As consciously as I can. In my acceptance and love of my alters, I have released many darker feelings that kept us separated. As I am still learning about my alters' lifesaving roles in my abuse history through continuous emerging memories, I discover aspects of buried emotions hidden within their essences. I must claim these feelings and occurrences, and reconnect the energy within myself. Once the charge is acknowledged, the disconnection happens quickly.

In addition, there are many people my Guides are helping me forgive/disconnect. In 1996, a divinely inspired journal writing created an experience of amazing power and tender forgiving with my mother. She has been dead since 1972 and was one of my main perpetrators. There was no way I had even considered letting her off the hook with my feelings of hatred and anger towards her as I experienced continuous memories of her violent abuse.

Two days after spending four hours with a healer, I wrote about the anguish of my mother's and my relationship. I saw how she projected all her pain and rage onto me, as an extension of herself and her unacknowledged inside people. There was nothing left of her core. She could never know who she was (an undiagnosed multiple) or receive the help she desperately needed, so she took her life.

While writing, I saw an image of Pandora's box. All the negative and evil feelings were opened and dumped on me. Yet, what remained at the bottom of the box was strength and hope. I needed to reclaim the box before it was reburied in the quicksand of my wounded ego where it would be difficult to surrender. A building energy shifted at that moment. My writing became poetic and my tears poured.

"Oh Ruby, such a life wasted, such a life destroyed, no way out and no way in. Bless your roving spirit. May it exit your hell and find peace among the light of Love. I release all debt we have between us now and forever more. There are no more cords that will bring us together nor keep us bonded. You are free from me, as I am from you. I cry, and I release you forever."

As I continue to "integrate the integration," I have chosen to consciously detach, not only from the dynamics of my family of origin, but from any connection with my biological family. This was actually a part of my forgiveness process. The question to stay in contact with the family members who act out the effects of the abuse emotionally, and stay in social connection with those who abused me, became clarified after many years of grief and inner debate. I no longer wanted to talk about the weather, having gone through one of the biggest transformations of my life. I wanted my authentic self to be present, at any given moment, without censorship.

In 1997, after listening to a tape by medical intuitive, Carolyn Myss, my Guides expanded on her message of individuating (becoming separate) from the family tribal membership. I felt it important to include my Guides' humorous, yet truthful, tribal membership rules that my biological family adheres to unconsciously. This information was pivotal in my decision to peacefully walk my own path, without the tribe, by totally ceasing all communication with them, and to move on with my life consciously. I feel this has been essential in honoring and loving all that I was, all that I am, and all that I will be, and trusting that my family is guided by the same Source that provides the healing in my life (if they choose to heal).

My family/tribal membership rules:
1) The Tribe supports all members in staying unconscious and codependent by use of alcohol, drugs, dissociation, blame,

manipulation, guilt, and abuse (any kind is acceptable).

2) If a Member moves towards interdependence and consciousness (including personal boundaries and truth-seeking confrontations), Tribe may use shaming, humiliation, ganging-up, talking behind one's back, lies, half truths, inventory-taking, and threats to coerce Member(s) back into the Tribe (Rule #1).

3) No one gets to tell the real family history—only censored or abridged version allowed.

4) Every Tribal Member is accepted no matter what dysfunctional action or heinous crime is involved as long as they still keep up a functional, outer appearance and accept the Tribal Rules. Thus, Members are supported in continuing tribal rule communications as stated in Rule #1.

5) By following the Tribal Rules, you are loved by the structure of the tribe (how it is set up) unconditionally. Remember—Family Tribal rules before personalities.

On a spiritual level, I view multiplicity as an archetype in my understanding of the Original Dissociation—being separated or dissociated from the Creator. There was One; out of ITS love to express, IT created the many in ITS image (of LOVE) to love, and gave them form. But as the many became entrenched in the world of matter and form, they forgot their Source; the dramas of their lives became their entire realities. They thought they were without the Creator's LOVE because they stopped identifying as the Creator's expression of LOVE. This illusion left them creating a reality of separation and disconnection from within themselves and from each other. Their fear of suffering in such spiritual and emotional isolation, and, oftentimes, physical pain, forced the many to eventually seek connection with each other, in order to establish safety (boundaries), to learn to trust, to communicate honestly, to connect intimately with a new awareness of love, and to become the expression of the Creator's Love. Then it came to their awareness, in that long journey, that they were always with and part of the Creator. Their beingness merged back with the One.

❧

Epilogue

There is still much to be revealed about the human body and psyche, and about their methods of survival and accommodation. If we visualize a circle and divide it into portions of "understanding," we might allot an eighth for "knowing what we know," a fourth for "knowing what we don't know;" the rest of the circle would represent what we "don't know about what we don't know."

The state of the outer world is a reflection of each individual's inner world, of its dissociation, its chaos, its diseases, and, for many, its healing. Our message of self-love and acceptance of all our parts, holds significance for those interested in bringing consciousness to both worlds. The planet has lived in fear of acknowledging and owning its dark, shadowy aspects. This covert and submerged energy creates tremendous pressure to project itself onto an unsuspecting world, and to use denial as truth, while, at the same time, withdrawing the conscious ability to take full responsibility for one's life. The shadow side must be brought up from its subterranean depths and recognized. Only then can it be dealt with. If we do not learn from our histories, the veil of darkness that is our pattern can arise even after integration. If this happens, have we, then, integrated life?

How many more wars will be fought, how much more blood fed into the increasingly infertile earth, how many more children deliberately starved and ill housed amidst wealth previously only dreamed about, before we gather the courage to face our history of brutal dissociation from the earth, from compassion for living things, from our inner wisdom, creativity, and spirituality? Cannot our divided, compartmentalized world be integrated, just as we multiples have been, with patience, work, and love?

Our greatest desire as human beings is to belong and to be loved. How can this occur if we do not engage in a continuing process of consciousness that connects us with all our feelings and provides the raw and, very often, dense, difficult materials to work with? Hard, thick clay (people)—when water (emotion) and touch (connection) are added—can be molded into a wonderfully pliable creation. But it takes love, commitment and work—inner and outer.

There are many people who have collectively made the decision to come together in awareness, understanding, and acceptance of who we *really* are: spiritual beings having sometimes dramatic human experiences. All of our experiences must be shared and given witness in order for us to heal. When the patterns of old, dysfunctional ways come into the Light, we learn that we were not alone in the perceived darkness of our shame, hatred, separation, and fear. We learn that as we let go of the old forms, change happens, new structures of consciousness manifest. We are all part of the process, a small part of a much grander system. It is our choice whether to flow with it unconsciously, or with awareness and integrity.

Judy Dragon, CHT, has been a Jin Shin Jyutsu® practitioner (hands-on healing art of energy balance) since 1979, later becoming a Clinical Hypnotherapist, teacher, writer and community educator. She is the mother of four children ranging in age from 15 to 22.

Terry Popp, Ph.D. is a writer. She teaches creative writing using mythology, fairy tales, films, and autobiography. She has a writing/editing consulting business, THE THIRD PATH.

Will Riggan, Ed.D., MFT, has a diverse background in public policy research, advocacy, university teaching, consulting, and psychotherapy. A member of the *International Society for the Study of Dissociation*, Dr. Riggan has presented at conferences and is presently preparing an article "Darkness and Flashes of Light: What the Phenomenon of DID Has to Tell Us About Ourselves."

Jonathan Rogers is a recovered survivor of severe childhood abuse. Earlier in his career he was an award-winning Hollywood animated film producer. During his recovery process, he saw images that portrayed how God's power protects and heals the human spirit. A catalog of Jonathan's artwork can be obtained by calling the Rogers Collection at 800-645-0114, or by writing c/o P.O. Box 598, Getzville, NY 14068.

Multiple Journeys to One
BOOK ORDER FORM

Date _____

ORDERED BY:

_____
Name and/or Agency

_____
Street address or P. O. Box

_____
City   State   Zip

(_____) _____ - _____
Daytime phone

SHIPPING ADDRESS (if different from above):

_____
Name and/or Agency

_____
Street address or P. O. Box

_____
City   State   Zip

Prices quoted in U.S. dollars:
  1–12 books — $17.95 each   •   13 or more — $14.95 each
Number of books _____ *@ (cost)* _____

Total cost of books	$ _____
Shipping and handling	$ _____
Special handling	$ _____
Subtotal	$ _____
California residents add 7.5%	$ _____
Total	$ _____

Make checks or money orders payable to **Dancing Serpents Press**
No cash or C.O.D., please. No returns.

Mail to:
Dancing Serpents Press, P. O. Box 8115, Santa Rosa, CA 95407-1115
E-mail: danserpents@juno.com

Shipping and handling (domestic):
  1 book: $3.00 fourth class; each additional book add $1.00
  1 book: $4.50 first class; each additional book add $2.00